THE
UNMEDICAL
MIRACLE

Oxygen

Elizabeth Baker, M.A.

PROMOTION PUBLISHING

Other Publications by Elizabeth Baker:
UNCOOKING: The Elizabeth Baker Story - Video
The GOURMET UNCOOK BOOK - Video
The UNCOOK BOOK
The UNDIET BOOK
The UNMEDICAL BOOK
The GOURMET UNCOOK BOOK

Warning - Disclaimer

The information in this book is presented as a matter of general interest only and not as prescribing cures. Readers must use their own judgement, consult a holistic medical expert or their personal physician for specific applications to their individual problems. The author and publisher assume no responsibility for error, inaccuracies, omissions or any inconsistency herein.

Library of Congress Cataloging-in-Publication Data

Baker, Elizabeth

   The UnMedical Miracle—Oxygen

Bibliography and Index.

ISBN: 1-887314-26-1

For information please contact:

Promotion Publishing
3368-F Governor Drive, Suite 144, San Diego, CA 92112
1 (800) 231-1776

Printed and bound in the United States of America

lst	Printing—1991	4th	Printing—1995
2nd	Printing—1992	5th	Printing—1996
3rd	Printing—1994		

Dedication

To all my countrymen who suffer, I dedicate this book of healing. May you seek and find, through faith, the knowledge you need to free your body, mind and spirit from the ills of this life. May you then fulfill the purpose God intended, having endowed you all with special gifts.

Foreword

As I was preparing to write this foreword, I was called by an investigative reporter from a Vancouver, B.C. newspaper, who was doing a story on the alleged persecution in Hong Kong of an alleged "crazy" advocate of the use of hydrogen peroxide to mitigate disease. I was shocked at his remark, "you must be kidding," when I said oxygen is our most critical nutrient and that this peroxide advocate might not be so crazy after all. Sadly, oxygen is taken for granted because unlike eating—we breathe unconsciously.

It is easy for us to conjecture a soldier in the trenches at the front at the end of a perilous supply line, which if interrupted, may cost him his life. But what about our cells? They, too, are like soldiers at the dead end of the supply line, and oxygen consumed constantly, must be constantly replaced or damage or cell death will occur (quickest in the brain and heart, more subtle elsewhere).

Oxygen delivery is not so simple. First, there must be adequate oxygen in the air. In our modern industrial, polluted, and enclosed environment, that is not always the case, as ambient levels may fall considerably. Additionally, there is scientific evidence that oxygen in the environment is actually on the decline and may have been as high as 30% many years ago. Oxygen must move across the lungs—a process impaired by any lung condition. There must be adequate red blood cell and iron stores to pick up the oxygen. The heart must efficiently move the blood, (impaired by hypertension, heart and vessel disease). The red blood cell must be flexible enough to squeeze through capillaries (the tiniest of blood vessels), which are actually smaller in diameter than the cells. Improper diet, especially toxic fats, such as is found in margarine, and lack of essential fatty acids, may impair red cell flexibility. The hemoglobin must give up its oxygen at the end of the line. But if the environment within the red cell is not right, the hemoglobin will actually retain the oxygen, depriving the awaiting cells. The oxygen, once released, must make a difficult journey across the capillary wall and extracellular fluid matrix. This process is hampered and impaired by toxic deposition in between cells from a heavily chemically-laden and synthetic diet. Arriving at the cell membrane, it must cross into the cell—a process again impaired by toxic fatty acids (margarine or plastic fat) in the cell membrane.

And finally, the cell must have the right nutrients in place to effectively "burn" the oxygen—a true rarity in today's modern "civilized" diet (the Standard American Diet). The pressure of oxygen in that final destination is only one-third of that in the lungs, if everything is working perfectly. Common sense suggests that even the slightest drop-off of that one-third pressure means big trouble. And trouble was proven by Otto Werberg in the 1920's, who won a Nobel Prize for showing cancer cells develop and grow, anaerobically, devoid of oxygen, fermenting sugar-like molds. And now we are seeing that all degenerative diseases, as well as the immune system's ability to fight pathogens, are directly impacted by the actual consumption of oxygen at the cellular level.

In this little book, you will learn of simple and inexpensive methods (hydrogen peroxide, ozone) to increase oxygen tension in the body. These therapies actually biochemically encourage and increase the release of oxygen by hemoglobin and turn on, or jump start, idle oxygen-consuming enzymes in the cells.

While many of us oxidative specialists have some reservations about the potential irritating effect on the stomach of hydrogen peroxide taken orally, the anecdotal reports of improvement of those who could tolerate it are most compelling. The use and results of ozone, more technical, but probably much better tolerated, borders on the unbelievable.

As a physician who has specialized in oxidative therapies for a majority of his years in practice, I encourage you to read on and learn how you can prevent or free yourself of the greatest risk factor to your health—oxygen starvation.

—Robert Jay Rowen, M.D.

Author's Foreword

They're almost too exciting to be true, those reports of hydrogen peroxide and ozone. Are we to believe them? I asked myself that question many times a few years ago as I began to read and hear about these uniquely capable substances and what they can do against disease. When I visited clinics in foreign countries and saw some of those miracles with my own eyes, I began a research project that ended with this book.

At first, I was doubting, cautious and skeptical. However, after seeing the multitude of research and clinical records dealing with oxygen and its two close relatives, hydrogen peroxide and ozone, I became convinced. Along with other recent books dedicated to bringing to light the truth that needs to be broadcast, this book takes its place. It calls out in a clear voice, "Wake up, Wake up! Oxygen equals life. There's abundant help for all who suffer."

Acknowledgements

When I do research in libraries, in clinical records and in my own bookshelves, I am ever grateful for the vast amount of work and commitment they represent. To all those unseen and unsung heros, thank you, thank you. To you wonderful, dedicated friends and coworkers who deserve the lion's share for getting out the all-important story of oxygen, my humblest gratitude, Arelim Steiner, R.N., Dorie Erickson, Brad Hunter B.S., Dan Williamson, George Freibott, M.D., N.D., Fanie Carriere, Lonni Erickson, Mark Sammons, Sonja Hargrove, ECHO Newsletter and the International Oxygen Therapy Association. How precious, persistent, long-suffering in many-houred days and nights you were! God bless you well.

Table of Contents

Introduction

First and foremost just what is oxygen? Oxygen is a gaseous element with the symbol 0. It is a colorless, odorless, tasteless gas. It is the most abundant element on earth, making up about half of the surface material. It makes up approxamately 90% of water, two-thirds of the human body and about 20% of air by volume. Normal atmospheric oxygen is made up of two molecules of oxygen (O_2). The most common reaction of oxygen in which it unites with other substances is called oxidation. So, what is oxidation? We know that no life can exist without oxidation. Oxidation is a chemical reaction. It is the process by which the body converts sugar into energy and helps rid the body of wastes. The body uses oxidation as its first line of defense against pathogens. The burning of a substance in air is rapid oxidation, rust is considered slow oxidation. Breathing of plants and animals is a form of oxidation.

This natural element, oxygen (O_2), is one of the four main elements of life—oxygen, hydrogen, nitrogen and carbon. While each of the elements is necessary for all forms of life, oxygen is the most conspicuously evident. We are often not consciously aware of it, but soon become aware when it is not there.

In recent years, ecologists, environmentalists, health advocates and the media constantly bring to our attention some phase of the status of oxygen in our world. Sufficient oxygen or lack of it is critical. Oxygen is the source of life and energy to all cells. Oxygen starvation or deficiency is probably the greatest cause of degenerative disease. Medical pioneers down through the years have been voicing this fact. Much of the time they have seen their words ignored and/or the outright shelving of their research records and publications.

The use of oxygen in therapy in the late 1920's and early 1930's was mainly put aside. Drugs became the way to treat the sick, although drugs never heal. They may relieve some suffering long enough for the body to heal itself. They do not help to eliminate the cause. They only treat symptoms. All drugs have side effects.

Oxygen treatment in the right concentration and amount has no negative side effects. It actually enhances the healing process. It improves and restores the immune system and may be the most significant single factor in prevention of illness. Oxygen is necessary for every cell, every tissue, every function, both chemical and physical, of the body. The bloodstream transports oxygen throughout the body to all the cells. Another role oxygen plays is its vital effect on two types of bacteria in the body, aerobic and anaerobic.

Aerobic bacteria are the friendly helpful ones in the body, in the water, in soil and in the air. Aerobic means, living or occuring only in the presence of oxygen. Aerobic bacteria are the normal flora of the body. They thrive on oxygen. They cannot live without oxygen.

Anaerobic microorganisms such as bacteria, make up the earth's bacteria of contamination, infection and disease. They live and thrive in impure food and in an unhealthy body. Anaerobic bacteria live in the absence of oxygen. They will die in the presence of it. Oxygen is nature's way of protecting mankind and all other forms of life by destroying the anaerobic bacteria that destroys man himself.

Oxygen is our most prevalent, abundant nutrient, yet the most overlooked and neglected one. Our purpose here is to bring it out in the open. We recognize the need to diffuse the knowledge of its place in the universe, of its role in life, health and recovery. We need to give it the prominence it so sorely deserves. Our goal is to reach the vast majority of people. Our wonderful yet ailing world needs the knowledge of this significant nutrient.

H2O2
What It Is

Chapter 1

H_2O_2 — What It Is

Of all the naturally occurring substances, one of the more controversial is Hydrogen Peroxide. One school of thought declares it to be of a profound healing nature. The other condemns it as something extremely hazardous that only the fool would try.

Just what is this substance around which so much controversy centers?

A peroxide is a chemical compound containing two oxygen atoms, each of which is bonded to the other and to some element other than oxygen, in this case it is hydrogen. It is an odorless, colorless, heavy, oxidizing liquid that has a very distinct taste. In hydrogen peroxide the atoms are joined together in a chain-like structure. Thus we have the elemental symbol H_2O_2. Peroxides are unstable and release oxygen when heated. In the body when hydrogen peroxide comes in contact with an enzyme in the blood (catalase), it breaks down the H_2O_2 into water and oxygen.

In nature H_2O_2 is formed by the action of sunlight in the atmosphere. This ultraviolet light splits an atmospheric oxygen molecule (O_2) into two single unstable oxygen molecules. These molecules then combine with others to form ozone or O_3. Ozone, being very unstable, readily gives up that one extra molecule of oxygen to rain water falling through this ozone layer to form hydrogen peroxide.

It is this H_2O_2 along with ozone that is nature's way of cleaning and re-oxygenating the air, water and soil of the earth. Due to the increased toxicity of the air, higher amounts of H_2O_2 react with these pollutants and so never reach the ground. This is why some farmers are now spraying crops with H_2O_2 diluted in water for increased crop yields, thus increasing the amount of oxygen that reaches the plants.

Hydrogen peroxide is believed by many to be harmful because of the increased formation of oxygen free radicals in the body. This has been the focus of much negative attention and incorrect science. It is blamed for many ailments people are experiencing today as well as premature aging. What we are not hearing is that the body itself produces and uses free radicals to attack and destroy harmful bacteria, viruses and fungi. It is the white blood cells in the body that make hydrogen peroxide for that specific purpose, fighting infection! It is also noted that lactobacillus found in the colon and vagina produce H_2O_2 for the same purpose of fighting the harmful bacteria and viruses that cause disease.

Hydrogen peroxide has had something of a bad reputation for being harmful or useless to the body. However, more recent research has revealed it as being a basic substance for good health and necessary for many biological reactions to occur all through our physical system. Let me note here that the very beginning of life provided us with high amounts of hydrogen peroxide as found in mother's milk, especially the very first milk (colostrum). It is generally known that Vitamin C helps fight infections by creating hydrogen peroxide. When taken internally, it dramatically raises the oxygen content of the blood and body tissues. Throughout the body it stimulates the production of enzymes, and helps in the function of many body systems. Although it is believed that there is no cure for emphysema, H_2O_2 therapy can offer relief and prevent severe complications that could cause death. The more we examine hydrogen peroxide the more we become aware of its effectiveness against so many destroyers of our health.

The biological purpose of hydrogen peroxide and ozone is to oxygenate the cells of the body and detoxify the blood. For this reason we must do all we can to protect and avoid deliberate depletion of them. It is disturbing to realize that the oxygen generating rain forests around the world are being destroyed at a rapid rate, causing a tragic reduction in the amount of oxygen available to all of us. We are being faced with a slow death due to oxygen starvation. The examples of oxygen depletion are endless. Such destruction translates to degenerative disease, the breaking down of the cellular structure of the body caused by a lack of life giving oxygen.

Curiously, many of the new nutritional supplements and natural remedies used for treatment of disease are effective because they get more oxygen to the cells. A good example is Co-enzyme Q10, effective for helping to regulate intercellular utilization of oxygen. Vitamins A, E, C, Beta-carotene, selenium and the element germanium as well as pycnogenol (a blend of bioflavonoids) enhance the transfer of oxygen to the cells of the body. Vitamin E is also taken to reduce the formation of free radicals in the body.

Below is a list of many conditions which have been and are being treated successfully with H_2O_2 therapy.

Allergies	Anemia
Arthritis	Asthma
Alzheimer's	Bronchitis
Altitude sickness	Bacterial infections
Cancer	HIV

Candida	Influenza
Cardiovascular Disease	Liver Cirrhosis
Diabetes type II	Lupus
Diabetic Gangrene	Multiple Sclerosis
Epstein-Bar Syndrome	Parasitic Infections
Emphysema	Parkinson's Disease
Fungus Infections	Periodontal Disease
Headaches	Ulcers
Herpes Simplex	Viral Infection
Herpes Zoster	Yeast Infection

In conclusion, the myriad services H_2O_2 performs in the body are it's availability, it's low cost, the simple ways it can be administered make it a miracle indeed. We are not saying everyone should take it or use it. There are doubtless those whose good health would not necessarily benefit by it's use. However, there are many whose health may be noticeably bettered, whose life might be prolonged and whose joy in living and serving can be greatly enhanced.

Ozone
The Noble Gas

Chapter 2

Ozone The Noble Gas

Just what is ozone? This intriguing question is sometimes wrongly answered. The element itself is frequently misunderstood.

Ozone is a blue gaseous form of oxygen with a pungent and penetrating odor, having the chemical symbol O_3. It consists of three atoms of oxygen instead of the more common two. It is derived or formed naturally from oxygen by an electric discharge or by exposure to ultraviolet radiation. It is a very *active* form of oxygen and is a very powerful oxidizer. Its various uses include water and air purification, disinfection, deodorization, bleaching and medical treatments for many diseases. Ozone is manufactured by passing dry air between two electrodes connected to an alternating high voltage.

The discovery of ozone dates back to 1785 when a scientist named M. Van Marum noted a peculiar odor in the air in certain atmospheric conditions. C.F. Schönbein in 1840 reported a new gas which he called ozone. However, not until 1872 was ozone identified and established as a substance having three atoms of oxygen.

Scientists and physicians the world over, are realizing ozone's great potential. Science and medicine have worked with ozone for more than 100 years. During World War II, Dr. Robert Mayer, treating German prisoners of war on Ellis Island, learned of medical ozone treatments from one of them. Since then he has given ozone therapy to patients in the United States, treating over 12,000 people successfully in 45 years of practice. He wrote many medical papers on the efficacy of this practice.

By 1973, Dr. Mayer and two other doctors had been granted 8 ozone patents, yet three years later the FDA stated in the Federal Register, "Ozone is a toxic gas with no known medical uses."

The FDA continues to maintain that about-face position despite overwhelming evidence to the contrary.

Medical, scientific and clinical reports from all over the world revealed, described and verified the effective use of ozone in most of the known diseases. Every month between 50 and 100 of these papers are published reporting positive results of treatment on diseases such as cancer, arthritis, multiple sclerosis, diabetes, heart disease, AIDS, Epstein Bar, hepatitis and many, many more. Yet in the United States, the government, medical hierarchy and media largely disparage or ignore the other world of effective modalities while millions needlessly suffer and die. If we remain silent, our caring, dedicated physicians, and therapists may have their natural therapies suppressed. Then big government and the giant drug industry can, more than ever, promote the use of drugs that harm, destroy and kill.

Facts Related to Ozone

Ozone is the most powerful form of oxygen. Ozone's only by-product is oxygen.

The oxygen you breathe has two molecules of oxygen.

Ozone has three molecules of oxygen and is known as triatomic oxygen.

Ozone is also known as activated oxygen. Ozone is natural, organic, and God-given.

Oxygen becomes activated when it encounters ultraviolet light and electrical energy.

Lightning creates ozone, as does sunshine.

Ozone is Nature's way of purifying the air we breathe and the water we drink.

Ozone is the strongest natural bactericide, fungicide, and viricide known to man.

Ozone has been used worldwide for over 100 years to purify water.

Ozone has been used to kill bacteria, fungi, and viruses in the body for over 75 years.

Ozone in the ozone layer protects us from harmful radiation from space.

Ozone is a powerful oxidant and can be harmful to your lungs when inhaled in high concentrations.

Ozone is present in automobile exhausts and in the smog in large cities. This ozone reduces hydrocarbons found in exhaust gases and smog by oxidizing them to carbon dioxide (CO_2) and water (H_2O).

Ozone is a very misunderstood and a very underapplied substance that could do much to decontaminate our environment and to relieve a multitude of the environmental and medical problems that we are suffering under.

Interesting Medical Ozone Facts

Ozone has been used in medicine at least since World War I.

Ozone disinfects open wounds.

Ozone purifies necrotic tissue and decubitus ulcers.

Ozone/Oxygen raises the PO_2 (oxygen pressure) of the blood.

Ozone oxidizes the lipid (fatty) layer of unhealthy infected cells and destroys them through a process called cell lysis (disintegration).

Since the 1920's, dentists have been using ozonated water to disinfect the mouth and stop bleeding.

Ozone has been proven to kill 100% of the viruses in donated blood samples.

Ozone forms peroxides and hydroxyperoxides when it encounters water in the blood.

Oncology researchers have reported a peroxide-ozone intolerance in tumor cells.

Lipid-containing viruses are sensitive to ozone; when their lipid layer is stripped through oxidation by ozone, they are effectively destroyed.

Viruses that are vulnerable to ozone because they are contained within lipid envelopes include: Herpes simplex, herpes zoster, Epstein Bar, influenza, mumps, measles, HIV, etc.

Ozone has been proven to inactivate the polio virus and Giardia cysts in drinking water and wastewater.

Ozone has been used to treat hepatitis, malaria, cholera, and dysentery with great success.

13

Ozone oxidizes fibrous tissue in veins and hemorrhoids, allowing them to shrink back to their normal size and recede into the tissue so that circulation is improved, and varicose veins and hemorrhoids may disappear.

Hemo-Ozonolysis has been used in Germany since the 1950's to disinfect donated blood and was found effective in eliminating transmission of hepatitis, syphilis, and HIV.

The majority of ozone treatments are received by otherwise healthy people as a means of revitalization, rejuvenation, and oxygenation, and as a preventive measure.

Ozone oxidizes the plaque in arteries allowing white blood cells to remove the break down products, and thus unclog arteriosclerotic arteries.

Superoxygenation

Chapter 3

Superoxygenation

What is the most important nutrient of all? It is oxygen. We can literally live for months without food, days without water but only minutes without oxygen. After about six minutes the brain starts to die.

Since oxygen is all important to life, it is reasonable to conclude that each of us should strive to be well oxygenated, or even superoxygenated. Otherwise, we cannot hope to have optimal health in today's world.

You may be saying, "Just what is meant by superoxygenation?" *Superoxygenation* means an abundance of oxygen made available to the cells of the body.

In explaining something of the utmost importance, we sometimes use the figurative expression, "It is the very life blood." Oxygen helps to keep that life blood alive, pure and clean to carry oxygen and other vital nutrients to every cell in the body for maintaining life and energy.

How then, can the system obtain this great abundance of oxygen? Fortunately the body can naturally take in oxygen three ways; through the lungs, through the skin and through the digestive system. Therapeutically, it can receive oxygen directly into the bloodstream by intravenous injection or by insufflation into the digestive tract. You may ask, "Air into the blood? I thought that caused injury, even death." Yes, air into the bloodstream is extremely dangerous. It can even be fatal because of the nitrogen in the air. But oxygen is infused into the blood in the form of ozone, a very active form of oxygen, as a gas, which upon contact with the bloodstream oxygenates the blood and begins to oxidize the toxins in the bloodstream. Ozone is a most effective oxygenator with **no** adverse side effects when used responsibly and with precise technology.

Optimal oxygen in the body gives vigorous health and vitality. Oxygen deficiency causes subnormal or ill health. If the deficiency is allowed to continue over a period of time, degenerative disease inevitably, subtly, follows. If a totally adequate supply of oxygen is made available to all the cells of our body, disease disappears. Well oxygenated cells do not get sick.

If oxygen is so all important, so protective against disease, so curative of disease, why hasn't the general public been informed? Why has oxygen treatment been neglected or withheld? Is it so new?

Actually, oxygen therapies have been around a long time. Hydrogen peroxide, H_2O_2, was discovered early in the 1800's. Ozone was first noticed in the mid 1700's and finally named as such in the latter part of the 19th century. Hydrogen Peroxide after that time was used as an antiseptic. Then a few years later a 3% solution was determined to be of satisfactory strength for a germicidal agent while not harming the skin. For decades, that solution of 3% hydrogen peroxide has been used as a mouth wash and as a disinfectant for home care, in clinics and in surgery.

Physicians have recognized for hundreds of years that fresh oxygen packed air helps to heal. Hippocrates advised his patients to breathe fresh air. All therapists realize it is conducive to health and prevention of disease not only with humans, but also with animals. Even in cold climates, farmers built cow and sheep sheds for exposure to fresh air by leaving the whole south side open to the weather. Chicken coops and houses had pens attached and extending from the open, sunny side. In such structures chickens avoided croup and other animals pneumonia. On my father's diversified wheat farm in northern Oklahoma where temperatures through the course of a year ranged from over 100 degrees to below zero, our poultry and animal shelters all had open southern exposures except the barn. That building usually had the upper half of the doors open for the circulation of air on those occasions when the horses were left inside. With green wheat fields in winter and buffalo grass pastures in summer for forage, our livestock were always healthy. I never remember a sick animal.

It has long been known that viruses travel only a very short distance in a well ventilated room, but quickly move clear across one closed off from sufficient ventilation. Added to that, air conditioning units are a veritable breeding ground for bacteria and virus, thus creating hothouses of communicable diseases.

Until the advent of sulfa and antibiotics, the treatment for tuberculosis (T.B.) consisted mainly of wholesome foods and absolutely fresh air twenty-four hours a day. When my grandmother was diagnosed as having "consumption," as T.B. was then called, Grandfather built her a screened porch outside their bedroom where she lived from mid February until her recovery early in the next November. Bed rest, abundant oxygen in the unpolluted air and wholesome, natural food cured her body of the dread disease.

From the late 1800's to the age of antibiotics in the late 1930's, there are clinical reports of the use of H_2O_2 from physicians successfully using it in addition to fresh air in treating diseases. Mostly these reports went unrecognized and unread by the medical profession. Over 6,000 articles on the effective, therapeutic use of H_2O_2 in the treatment of disease have been found and correlated, a work started by Dr. Edward Carl Rosenow (1875-1966). Walter Grotz and Father Richard Willhelm, two of the most influential men in the crusade to let people know of the beneficial effects of hydrogen peroxide therapy, carried on Dr. Rosenow's works. In 1987, the two were recipients of the Pioneer Award in Medicine given by the National Health Federation. Walter Grotz continues to speak on the benefits of the self administration of H_2O_2. This simple treatment is literally saving lives, improving health and giving hope to people who have been told there was no hope for them.

It is with great sadness that we note here the passing of Father Richard Willhelm on September 20, 1993. Father Willhelm was a leading pioneer in the use of hydrogen peroxide for the treatment of disease and in the recovery of health.

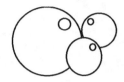

What Can Happen When Oxygen Is In Short Supply?

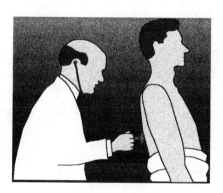

Chapter 4

What Can Happen When Oxygen Is In Short Supply

To remain healthy, every cell in the body has to have a continuous, optimal supply of oxygen. When that oxygen is in short supply, changes begin to take place in the cell. It does not perform normally and its function is impaired. All of the physical and chemical processes of the body require oxygen. It is necessary to maintain a balanced system and to purify the blood. But most importantly, our body uses oxygen to rid itself of toxins and disease causing organisms. If a diminished supply of oxygen were to continue, carbon monoxide (CO) is formed in the blood. Carbon monoxide is not easily eliminated and because of its toxic nature, cell degeneration begins and that leads to trouble. Carbon monoxide is a de-oxidizer which causes the body's immune system to weaken, thus allowing various pathogens to invade, the result being disease.

What is the disease that starts? What determines which disease may proliferate? And in what part of the body?

We have all heard the old saying, "A chain is only as strong as its weakest link." True. Our bodies all may have a weak link or links. Given optimal oxygen, even the weak links can continue to function adequately for a long, long time. But given a minimum supply, dysfunction or breakdown of the weak part or area results and we have the beginning of a trouble spot. With one person that weak spot may be kidneys. With another it could be the skin (the body's largest organ), or the heart, or the immune system, or the digestive tract, or the liver, or the eyes. Even a partial lack of oxygen translates to weakened performance on the part of the cells. Coupled with deficiencies of minerals, enzymes and vitamins, that oxygen poor area of the body is in real trouble when a scarcity of oxygen compounds the deficiency problems. Drugs, surgery, synthetic *nutrients,* manipulation, hormones, etc., cannot correct the cause which in today's world is frequently deficiencies of the right kinds of food and too little oxygen. Restore the oxidative process and the situation will be normalized.

Remember, oxygen is our most vital nutrient. A skimpy supply of it can cause the first weak spot of the body to become vulnerable to disease. Remember, disease proliferates where cells receive *insufficient oxygen.* Diseased cells—cancer, M.S., diabetes, psoriasis, Parkinson's, AIDS, heart disease, phlebitis, emphysema, etc.—are anaerobic cells. That means they thrive where there's little or no oxygen.

Why don't we get enough oxygen? What can happen to shortchange us with this nutrient that is everywhere in our environment and free for the taking?

How tragic that the air most of us breath is lacking in its full quota of oxygen. Pollution from industry, asphalt paving, car emissions, wood stoves, chemical plants and so on *ad infinitum,* destroy oxygen. Household cleaning products, solvents, paints, polyester drapes and bedding, synthetic perfumes and cosmetics lower the oxygen supply in our homes as do air conditioners and electric appliances. We prevent our skin from absorbing as much oxygen as it should by wearing clothing of synthetic fabrics. We work in hermetically sealed buildings where health-giving, oxygen-supporting, negative ions trickle in through an air conditioning system. This system is woefully lacking in capacity or performance for providing an adequate supply of oxygen. And we ride home in cars upholstered with synthetic fabrics that gas off and contribute to oxygen poor city smog and car exhaust. The home prepared meal or the *good* restaurant foods we look forward to at the end of our day is oxygen depleted because it is mostly cooked. This means no oxygen or enzymes remain to help us digest and assimilate the meal. And because so much of the nutrition in the food has been destroyed, our bodies are left still craving food. In spite of this, we eat on and on until we overindulge, a prevalent habit that should have more oxygen instead of less, for the food to be digested properly. The result is similar to water dripping slowly on the head of a bound prisoner to produce a slow demise. Overeating of oxygen-poor, nutrient-deficient, cooked and processed food is slow, torturous death.

As the years pass, first one problem then another starts appearing. We carry on in a lifestyle that we think best suits us. We are so comfortable with our old habits we think they are right. If something goes wrong, we can always see a doctor. There are countless miracle drugs and plenty of *good* hospitals, clinics and specialists. Not to worry. All bases are covered. Anyway, nothing will happen to us.

Then illness strikes. One person has a heart attack. Another a stroke. Yet another's problem of sudden weight loss is leukemia; another's knees have gone bad and the doctors say operate to see what is wrong.

We all ask ourselves the question, "Why?" Who will tell us the truth? Who is there to proclaim all that good, wonderful tasting, delicious, beautiful food we've been eating gives us mostly ill health? Who can convince us that we've overeaten most of our lives, that we've actually starved our bodies of essential nutrients while overstuffing them with dead, overcooked, greasy foods, artificially colored, artificially flavored and saturated with preservatives?

Certainly not many doctors are going to tell you your body is starving for nutrients, especially oxygen. If they did, they might have a difficult time convincing you. And if they don't tell you, chances are it's because they don't *know or believe* it. Most physicians practicing today have never studied nutrition, or health, or prevention, or basic disease cause. They study anatomy, disease, diagnosis, surgery and drugs. True, an encouragingly increasing number are turning to nutrition, with a real awareness of the need for more oxygen, among other nutrients. Even though the increase of such doctors is 10% to 15% more over the year before, the total number is discouragingly small for helping the sickest nation in the world improve its health. The answer is for each of us to take responsibility for our health in our own hands and learn alternate ways of maintaining health and treating disease.

It is amazing to me to hear how many people sleep with windows closed and rarely if ever make the effort to completely air out their houses. Airing out the house, hanging the bedding on the line, washing the curtains and wiping down the walls with hydrogen peroxide was a custom my grandmother and my mother faithfully followed seasonally. My grandmother used to say she slept much better after the cleaning ritual, had more energy and felt better. As a youngster, I considered myself victimized by this "nuisance" custom and took grandmother's words as "all in her mind."

Now I realize that grandmother was right. She cleaned out the dust, the mites, the mold and filled the bedding and the house with oxygen fresh air and sunlight. I doubt if grandmother knew she put an extra charge of oxygen into the house with the hydrogen peroxide she used to kill germs. But now I realize she really did feel better, and for a reason. Extra oxygen, taken in naturally, does give us more energy and makes us feel better, calmer and more at peace.

In the 1970's when carpeting was made of polyester, a young couple we knew moved into their new 7 room house. It was carpeted throughout, even the bathrooms and kitchen. At the house warming party for them, I had to leave early. The gas-off of the polyester carpeting was so poisonous for me I lost my speech temporarily. A few weeks later in mid-winter the young couple and their two small children were all sick. The husband had asthma, the wife no energy and lived with a headache, one child had a constant runny nose and the other bronchitis and a skin rash.

When the grandmother took me by to see them, we recoiled at the stale, oxygen poor, toxin laden atmosphere of the house. Our advice to the desperate young mother's plea for help was to the point. Put on a lot of extra clothing, turn off the heat, throw open the windows and spray the entire house—ceilings, walls, drapes, furniture and carpeting—with three percent hydrogen peroxide. In a few days they were all improved.

The water we drink in our world today has far less oxygen than in former times. When we put chlorine and fluoride in drinking water we further deplete the oxygen.

Before mankind polluted the atmosphere, rain water falling though the ozone layer brought extra oxygen to the earth in the form of hydrogen peroxide.

This cleansing, purifying, refreshing, oxygen containing substance is essential to the very life and health of us all.

There isn't as much oxygen available to us in the air we breathe today. We must all, individually and collectively, make the effort to get more oxygen into our systems in every way possible.

27

There are yet more reasons why many people do not get enough oxygen. When bad odors or smog or dust or other noticeable toxins are present in the air, we naturally breathe more shallowly. The more shallow our breath, the more we lose lung capacity for breathing. This is especially bad for the very young whose bodies should have a clean air environment for growth and development, as well as the elderly. The latter, frail and lacking exercise, are already at a disadvantage for receiving oxygen because of diminished lung capacity (5% to 15% less than normal).

Last but certainly not least, is vigorous exercise which forces us to pull great quantities of air into our lungs for the maintenance and rejuvenation of our bodies. I know a lady who after a two year illness and very little physical activity, learned her lung capacity was fifteen percent below normal (average). Shocked, she determined to do something about it. Friends told her of a retired lung specialist teaching breathing exercises. After attending his classes and doing the exercises for only a few days, she felt and slept better. And at the end of a year her lung capacity was only three percent below normal instead of fifteen percent.

Oxygen deficiency is so widespread, so universal, it is of the utmost importance to know the reasons why we may not be getting enough. To summarize:

Air pollution

Processed foods

Cooked foods

Smoking

Chemically treated water

Polluted water

Sprayed fruits and vegetables

Toxin polluted homes

Lack of ventilation in offices, work places and homes

Lack of exercise

It takes some doing but each of us can increase his/her oxygen intake. The best start is improving the diet which is discussed in Chapter 10.

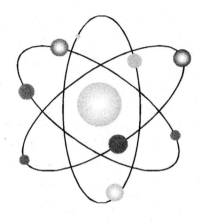

Why Oxygen Can
And Does Cure

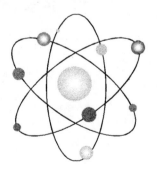

Chapter 5

Why Oxygen Can And Does Cure

The word *cure* has fallen into ominous circumstances. Laws and regulations have been passed against its usage in some places. As a result, people are suspicious of it and avoid using it. They distrust those who have the courage to use it and can still verify the truth of the word with its full meaning. However, there is a time and occasion when it needs to be used.

When we suffer a wound and perhaps resultant infection then experience the return to our normal condition and function, we say we are healed. The cut or infection is no more. When the ordeal is over, the spot where the wound\infection completely recovered is restored, what word better expresses the cycle than cured?

Oxygen therapies are actually *curing,* healing, ending many diseases. However, most people are timid about choosing the word to describe the total absence of the disease. They deem it unethical or unwise or they fear rejection even on the part of their non-medical listeners. The conventional medical profession actually displays some hostility to the word. Is it any wonder? In their practice they sometimes see improvement, occasionally they see remission but rarely, if ever, do they see cure of degenerative disease short of a miracle. They seldomly admit to *cure* and only then with strong reservations.

Recently, medical scientists in a number of countries have found that cells of all the degenerative diseases thus far researched are anaerobic, **without oxygen**. In other words, degenerative disease cells proliferate only where cells get little or no oxygen. Healthy cells live and thrive as long as adequate oxygen and good nutrition are supplied to them. Reduce that supply and the cells become "puny," as one able researcher termed it. "They change. Are distorted. They themselves degenerate and those around them do the same."

All normal body cells meet their energy needs by respiration of oxygen, whereas cancer cells meet their energy needs in great part by fermentation. All normal body cells are thus obligate aerobes, whereas all cancer cells are partial anaerobes. In cancer, oxygen as an energy enhancer has been replaced by an energy yielding reaction of the lowest living forms, namely, a fermentation of glucose. In any case, during the cancer development the oxygen respiration always fails and fermentation appears. What remains are growing machines that destroy the body in which they grow.

Remember: Where cells get enough oxygen, cancer will not, cannot occur. —*Otto Warburg,* Lindau, Germany, 1966.

In the majority of cases, an oxygen poor, nutritionally deficient diet has been the single most direct cause of degenerative disease. The most direct and effective way out of that disease is an abundance of oxygen and an all natural, mostly all raw diet. Let me say here that to get maximum benefit of the oxygen, you must have the necessary mineral compliment in the body to carry the oxygen to the cells. Minerals are critical to the utilization of oxygen in the body. A decrease of minerals will increase the load of detoxification on the oxygen supply that already exists.

How does one get more oxygen to the cells? For correcting a degenerative condition in the body, oxygen in the form of hydrogen peroxide or ozone, in very dilute solution or gas, administered by intravenous injection or by insufflation is the most effective, therapeutic way.

Oxygen can be used in the form of 35% food grade hydrogen peroxide greatly diluted by pure water and taken by the glassful several times a day. (See Appendix)

A practical, easy way to get oxygen into the body is by putting hydrogen peroxide in bath water, daily or weekly. Depending on the urgency and the frequency of treatments, from one to ten pints of 3% hydrogen peroxide can be put in a bathtub half filled with warm water or one half cup of 35% food grade. The person then bathes in it for twenty minutes to half an hour.

Extra oxygen can be helped into the body by rubbing 3% H_2O_2, on the skin—arms, legs, body, face and neck. Straight 3% hydrogen peroxide makes a germicidal mouthwash and throat gargle. It is another way to get extra oxygen into the system. While cleansing the mouth and throat, it destroys the bad bacteria there and strengthens and improves the health of the gums. It also helps to clear up periodontal disease, helps remove plaque from teeth and clean off the coating of the tongue.

Here's how one may use it. On arising in the morning, rinse out the mouth with water, then scrape the tongue with a spoon. Scrape far back on the tongue, making yourself gag. This causes a deep cough which brings up phlegm and a quantity of bacteria out of the throat. After scraping the tongue several times, rinse mouth with water then wash and gargle with 3% hydrogen peroxide for one half to one minute, allowing the solution to bathe under the tongue. A bit of oxygen will be absorbed directly into the bloodstream, which carries it to all parts of the body. After spitting out the mouth wash, allow the tiny bit of remaining hydrogen peroxide to continue working on the bacteria of the mouth. You will find that a fine coating of tiny white bubbles (foam) will coat your mouth and tongue. It's the H_2O_2 doing its work against the bacteria. Rinse mouth well after a minute or so. Many find H_2O_2 to be a superior healing antiseptic that contributes more to health than any of the regular mouth washes on the market today.

Other than breathing, the greatest way to get oxygen into the cells of our bodies is through uncooked, living foods where the necessary nutrients are stored. All the building materials are there. All maintenance and energy essentials are there. Oxygen is there. It alone in a nutrient deficient body is a great, lifesaving substance. However, for recovery and overall physical and mental function we need the complete nutrition that is immediately available to us in all living foods.

We destroy from 30% to 85% of the nutrients in foods when we cook them. Vitamins C and B6 are almost totally destroyed by boiling. Most of the other vitamins are partially destroyed. The high temperatures of frying, broiling and baking not only destroy the nutrients, they alter the fat so drastically it is not digestible. This ruined fat clogs the bloodstream and the arteries. Fats heated to high temperatures go through a brief period of rancidity before they reach a bake-out temperature of 350-400 degrees Fahrenheit. Not only is the food value of such fats ruined, the fat itself becomes a very harmful substance, contributing to oxygen deficiency, phospholipid deposits in the blood vessels and a rubbery plaque on the intestinal walls. **These coatings prevent the intestines from normal absorption of nutrients, including oxygen**.

Boiling, frying, steaming and baking foods destroy most or all of the oxygen. They also destroy all enzymes which are necessary for the digestion and absorption of foods.

From what has been discovered so far, we know that degenerative diseases can proliferate anywhere cells are oxygen starved. And by researching the well documented records of physicians in the United States, Europe and Mexico, we learn of remissions of degenerative diseases after oxygen therapy: cancer, diabetes, heart disease, multiple sclerosis, tumors—malignant and benign, AIDS, Epstein Bar, candida albicans, Parkinson's disease, lupus, psoriasis, colitis, etc.

Scientists and physicians for ages have searched for the basic physical cause of disease. With what has been known and practiced for well over a hundred years, it is quite apparent that a lack of oxygen and/or poor oxygen transport to the cells is certainly a basic deficiency. **It is primary**. Therefore, it is entirely reasonable, in view of the generally recognized fact, to assume insufficient oxygenation may be a primary cause of degenerative disease.

If this is the case, then it logically follows that proper, optimal oxygenation can prevent and even reverse degenerative disease. A body that is well oxygenated, free of toxins and with the full compliment of minerals and proper nutrition, can live disease free for a very long time.

The concept is simple. Oxygen therapy is simple. So simple that all oxygen therapies, except I.V. infusions of hydrogen peroxide or ozone, can be carried on by the individual person or their home care professional. Oxygen in this form is cheap, it is painless and it is readily available to all because it is not a prescription drug. It is not a drug at all. And there are no toxic side effects if done properly.

In spite of the abundance of clinical evidence of the effectiveness of these therapies, H_2O_2, and O_3 are unrecognized or at worst, deliberately ignored by the medical profession. Over 6,000 medical papers on the use of hydrogen peroxide were peer researched. Some of these articles appeared in the 1800's. Many appeared in the 1920's and early 1930's. Any number have appeared in the last decade or two. The researchers who reviewed the articles, Walter Grotz and Father Richard Willhelm, have been honored for their outstanding contribution to medical science. They were also honored for alerting the public to the need for breaking the strangle hold of the medical profession on sick care and on health care today.

Without these two men who have done so much to provide this nation with the information on the beneficial effects of oxygen, we would undoubtedly be in a sorrier state of affairs.

Oxygen Therapy And
Bio-Oxidative
Treatment

Chapter 6

Oxygen Therapy
Bio-Oxidative Treatment

Oxygen can enter the cells of our bodies in three ways. For clarity we list them specifically:

Lungs—the most oxygen is taken in by the breath to the lungs.

Skin—This largest of organs readily absorbs a part of the substances coming in contact with it. Oxygen is one of those substances.

Digestive Tract—The oxygen naturally present in uncooked foods is perfectly assimilated by the body. It is essential for oxygen to be in the digestive system for optimal health, healing, prevention and recovery of degenerative disease and for providing a healthful environment in the intestines for the beneficial flora.

Fresh, clean air plays a major role in maintaining health and in bringing about recovery from sickness and injury. Tragically, those who live in large cities suffer an insufficient supply. Oxygen levels in the air may be down to as much as 10% in some heavily industrialized cities. Add to this, toxic odors in the air which encourage shallow breathing. Living in an environment of oxygen poor, pollutant-saturated air also causes people to neglect sufficient exercise. Together these two results of polluted air cause the lungs to lose some of their capacity to take in oxygen, which in turn starts deterioration in health. A vicious circle is set up: the less oxygen the lungs take in because of pollution and lack of exercise, the less oxygen they are capable of taking in for maintaining health.

The most amazing, dramatic method of treating a prolonged case of oxygen deficiency leading to such degenerative diseases as prostate and breast cancer, diabetes, hypoglycemia and a low immune system is hydrogen peroxide or ozone therapy. These natural, antimicrobial agents cure the "incurables." At the last professional count, it was learned that many doctors and naturopaths in the United States are successfully using O_3 and H_2O_2. In Europe and Mexico, thousands of people have been treated with millions of treatments of these same oxygen therapies. These trained physicians have formed an organization known as the **International Oxidative Medicine Association.** They provide an international reference list of physicians. (Write to IOMA, P.O. Box 891954, Oklahoma City, OK 73189. Phone (405) 634-1310. Fax (405) 634-7320. This organization spreads the word of the effectiveness of hydrogen peroxide. It provides an update of technical procedures and refinements for doctors who use intravenous H_2O_2 therapy on their patients. To get around the outmoded, restrictive regulations of the FDA, these doctors classify their therapies as experimental. How long that can go on is anyone's guess. We hope and pray in the meantime that the public **demand** through media exposure will start a nationwide movement for official approval of hydrogen peroxide in treatments.

In his book, *"The Therapeutic Use of Intravenous Hydrogen Peroxide,"* Dr. Farr discusses the curative effects of H_2O_2. First of all, it kills virus, bacteria, protozoa and yeast. It stimulates oxidative enzymes. It restores elasticity to the walls of the arteries. It oxidizes (dissolves) lipids (fats) from arterial walls. It dilates heart vessels naturally and without side effects. It strengthens oxygen tension intracellularly. It improves and regulates cellular membrane transport of oxygen.

These substances, ozone and hydrogen peroxide, help conquer disease and restore the body's oxygen to a healthy level. The process is so simple it is generally unbelieved by those in orthodox medicine. Hydrogen peroxide (H_2O_2) and ozone (O_3) have been around so long they are commonplace and overlooked. In concentrated form they are highly oxidative. Yet extremely diluted in an I.V. or through insufflation they work miracles.

Hydrogen peroxide is put directly into the vein, usually along with other bio-supportive nutrients and/or substances. Depending on the severity of the disease, the patient receives an I.V. infusion from two times a day to twice a week. They usually begin to improve with the first infusion and feel better with each succeeding one. Ozone is also administered in a similar way through rectal insufflation, which puts the ozone into the digestive tract. From there it is absorbed directly into the bloodstream.

An early way of using ozone was by drawing a pint of blood from the patient, injecting it with ozone, then transfusing the blood back into the patient. This is a very revealing process because the blood turns a bright red on contact with the ozone. All impurities and toxins are neutralized and the blood is made pure. As with the H_2O_2 treatment, the patient receiving his own purified blood immediately improves.

Some physicians put the highly diluted ozone directly into an I.V. with the same beneficial results. Sometimes, along with the dilute ozone and other nutrients, they inject DMSO into the I.V. solution. DMSO has the marvelous quality of rendering the ozone and other nutrients more effective.

How tragic are infections from catheters in the bladder and which then may be multiplied in the drainage bag. They can cause a multitude of complications and even death from infection. Hydrogen peroxide in the bag can prevent this problem by keeping the tube and drainage bag sterile of bacteria. (30 milliliters of three percent H_2O_2, will keep the urine bag bacteria free for eight hours according to Dr. William C. Douglass, M.D.)

Oxygen therapy has been around a long time in hospitals and clinics in the form of an inhalable gas (O_2). However, it is not recommended as a source of supplemental oxygen for day to day living. It's an emergency treatment. A maximal amount of oxygen quickly given is all right for a boost when immediate oxygen is distressfully insufficient for the patient or even life threatening.

Hyperbaric oxygen or hyperbaric ozone treatments are another way of getting oxygen into the body. This also is an emergency treatment. It is very expensive and not advisable or practical for a long term, natural therapy for recovery and maintaining optimal oxygenation of the body. Hyperbaric oxygen/ozone therapy calls for a chamber where the patient is placed and subjected to pressure to force oxygen/ozone into the bloodstream. It can be lifesaving especially in smoke inhalation, burns, cyanide poisoning and carbon monoxide poisoning. The hyperbaric oxygen/ozone equipment costs around $100,000 a unit. By comparison, hydrogen peroxide or ozone costs a few pennies to a few dollars.

The wonderful thing about the other oxygen therapies is that they can usually be self administered and carried on at home.

By putting from one to ten pints of 3% H_2O_2 in an average size bathtub half full of warm water, anyone can oxygenate, strengthen, energize and rehabilitate his/her body by soaking in it for twenty or thirty minutes.

Hot tubs and pools become health rejuvenators and disease fighters when treated with hydrogen peroxide or ozone instead of chlorine which is a real danger. Chlorine destroys vitamins and other beneficial factors in the body as it is absorbed through the skin into the bloodstream. It also destroys oxygen in the body.

In our 170 gallon jacuzzi, which is kept at about 103 degrees, we add 2 or more cups of 35% percent Food grade Hydrogen peroxide every three days. Fatigue disappears after a ten or fifteen minute soak in it. We emerge feeling renewed and uplifted because of the extra oxygen that we have absorbed through the skin. It has been shown that a 200 pound person can absorb up to 4 pounds of water in a 20 minute soak in a hot bath.

Three percent H_2O_2 can be rubbed on the skin, a good way to help improve the oxygen balance of the body. A couple in their early seventies took oxygen therapy along with an all natural, mostly raw diet for her Epstein Bar and cancer and his high blood pressure and asthma. Both recovered. Now in their late seventies, they maintain vigorous, problem free health. They exercise daily, eat a cleansing diet of living foods and rub their entire bodies with half strength 3% hydrogen peroxide nearly every day. Their energy and good humor testify to the effectiveness of their lifestyle.

An acquaintance wrote us that for family colds, he puts four ounces of 35% H_2O_2 in a gallon of water in his children's humidifier. After a night's sleep with this running in the bedroom, most if not all symptoms are relieved!

The most practiced of the H_2O_2 therapies is perhaps the simplest of all: taking it in purified drinking water. Thousands of people around the world testify to the health benefits received as a result of oral H_2O_2 on a regular basis.

For treatment of specific diseases or problems, some people increase the dosage gradually. The hydrogen peroxide liberates free oxygen as it contacts pathogens (bacteria and virus) in the stomach where levels of streptococcus and virus are high. This may cause gas and/or a feeling of nausea. In such a case, many find that eating a piece of fruit thirty to forty-five minutes later relieves the symptoms. Also mixing the H_2O_2 with aloe vera juice may offset this problem. Some people buy ordinary drugstore USP (pharmaceutical grade) 3% hydrogen peroxide for the oral oxygen treatment. Such H_2O_2 is considered unsafe to ingest in water or fruit juice, as it does contain chemical stabilizers in it. However, **35% food grade** H_2O_2 is recommended for internal treatment. A pint of 35% food grade contains the equivalent of 130 pints of oxygen. A pint of 3% H_2O_2 contains 10 pints of oxygen. Since 35% is a dangerous, very strong solution, it must be carefully diluted. The treatment often used is as follows: 1-3 drops 35% H_2O_2 in a glass of water three times a day then increased a drop per dose each day to 8 or more drops or whatever you feel comfortable with. A total of 25 drops 1-3 times a day in cases of degenerative diseases may be advisable until the problem is in remission. Patients afflicted with candidiasis are advised to start with only one drop per dose. (See appendix for sources of more information and details.)

Hydrogen peroxide available in various strengths and grades, is noted here for purposes of general information:

3% pharmaceutical grade: This is sold in local drugstores and supermarkets. Not recommended for internal use.

35% food grade: This is used in the production of foods such as cheese, eggs etc. **This is the only grade recommended for internal use.**

In spite of thousands of people who have taken and are continuing to take therapeutic hydrogen peroxide with no problems, controversy still lingers over the practice. There are people who have an adverse digestive reaction. Some doctors feel the risk of an irritated stomach from an imbalanced *pH* (due to excess hydrogen), is not worth the chance taken to cure a disease. They prefer to give the H_2O_2 or O_3 by I.V. or insufflation where there are no unfavorable reactions when proper dilutions are precisely given.

With all of these wonderfully effective treatments, there remains what has been and still is the most effective and lasting therapy yet: natural nutrition of living fruits, vegetables, seeds and nuts, discussed in Chapter 9.

Raw foods still have all their vitamins and minerals, enzymes and oxygen. In cooked foods, vitamins are mostly destroyed, minerals thrown away, enzymes killed and oxygen boiled, baked or broiled off. Cooked foods are dead foods. Dead food cells can no longer transfer their life force to living cells. We cannot expect to maintain radiant health and activity for any great length of time by feeding our bodies with dead, nutritionless, oxygen poor, processed, artificial, chemicalized foods.

I.V.'s, baths, insufflation, ingestion and massages of hydrogen peroxide constitute emergency measures for coping with and treating degenerative disease. But for recovery followed by continued, disease free, optimal health, an all natural diet of mostly raw, live foods must be adhered to as a way of life.

For the reader's convenience, we summarize here the several bio-oxidative treatments and therapies:

Intravenous use of H_2O_2, (hydrogen peroxide)

Intravenous and insufflation use of O_3 (ozone)

Air purifiers

Hyperbaric oxygen/ozone

Oral use of hydrogen peroxide, as a highly dilute oxygen water

Ozonated water for drinking H_2O_2 or ozone in bath or hot tub

Ozone generators for home air purification

One last but not least oxygenation factor in the total health care concept is exercise. Our bodies were made for action—work, play, service, movement, activity. The familiar saying, "If you don't use it, you lose it," is old because it is true. Exercise—walking, swimming, jumping rope, gardening, tennis, golf, yoga, tai chi, jogging, aerobics, calisthenics, and so on and on. Exercises keep us breathing deeply to get out the bad air, pull in the good, thus oxygenating our bodies. Exercise, almost on a par with diet, must not be neglected if we are to enjoy continued good health or health regained after conquering disease. Exercise is not only essential to good health of the body but to the mind and the spirit as well.

Hydrogen Peroxide And Ozone

In Nature,
Agriculture
and Industry

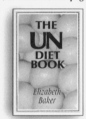

Videos From
Elizabeth Baker

UnCooking: The Elizabeth Baker Story
featuring: ELIZABETH BAKER $24.95+S&H / 45 min.

Best selling author, Elizabeth Baker, in this informative interview, shares her story of overcoming terminal illness after conventional medicine had given up on her. Her thorough and painstaking research in health and nutrition led to fascinating discoveries about the harm of processed foods. Mrs. Baker's methods of preparing and eating raw, unprocessed foods are so simple, anyone can become the epitome of health. Her unique and refreshing ideas result in an exceptional video experience.

The Gourmet UnCook Book
featuring: ELIZABETH BAKER $12.95+S&H / 30 min.

Elizabeth Baker teaches us the true value of eating well without feeling deprived with her emphasis on raw, unprocessed foods. Mrs. Baker shares her story of overcoming cancer and Addison's disease following the nutritional guidelines she researched and designed herself. Try some of Elizabeth Baker's easy-to-prepare, delicious gourmet recipes and preparation techniques and you too, can obtain abundant energy and optimum health.

Chapter 7

Hydrogen Peroxide And Ozone In Nature, Agriculture And Industry

When hydrogen peroxide is mentioned, most people think of the drugstore variety that bubbles and fizzes its way through the bacteria of a fresh cut or small surface infection. Many a childhood tear has been stopped as the young sufferer of a cut or skin scrape watches the bizarre and entertaining action as hydrogen peroxide does it's work. Although the use of H_2O_2 is no longer commonplace in our personal experiences today, it is still usual and natural in our outdoor environment.

Rain and snow falling through the ozone layer of our atmosphere produces hydrogen peroxide. It is an abundant lifegiver. It is this *oxygen* freshness that boosts our physical energy, gives a clearer mind and spiritual uplift. We feel better. In our world today many populated areas are robbed of this experience because pollution has robbed the oxygen from our atmosphere. The result is less oxygen in the environment available to us, which translates to less energy and ill health.

Waterfalls and streams that run white are cleansed of microbes and germs because the agitation of water over rocks and gravel creates added oxygen. Many of us learned from our rural upbringing or our scout and camping days that such white water was safe to drink. It was safe because of the purifying presence of oxygen.

By vigorously shaking a bottle of water for several seconds, we can increase its oxygen content enough to improve the taste and purity.

There are other phenomena in nature that contribute to pure water. Freezing improves the taste, quality and purity of water. As children, we loved to break icicles from the cattle watering tank and chew or suck on them. They were *safe,* as our parents said. As a matter of fact, one way to have better oxygenated water is to drink water from melted ice.

For hundreds of years, people have flocked to health spas. There natural, *healing* water shot up from artesian wells, or bubbled out of rocks near the foot of a mountain, or cascaded down the crevasse of a bluff into a sparkling white fall or gushed over a naturally terraced river bed to a whirling pool of bubbled, clean, rejuvenating water. All such places were correctly recognized as possessing some healing quality.

In the 16th century, Ponce de Leon set out on his hazardous journey to search for the fountain of youth. Since ancient times in Spain, and other old world countries, a courtyard fountain with its ornate beauty and the soothing sounds of cascading water, has been known to be restful and healthful. People truly felt better around the fountain and drinking its water. It was more than psychological. It actually physically helped. Healing water spas have been popular for centuries.

One such famous healing spa is near Lourdes, France. So many testimonies of cures and recovery from illness have persisted that literally hundreds of thousands of pilgrims seeking a miraculous deliverance from illness go there. Of course they are healing. These are spring waters from high mountain snow melt. They are complete with extra oxygen.

The famous Japanese scientist, Dr. Asai, who cured his own throat cancer in the 1960's with germanium, a then little known mineral which helps the body conserve and transport oxygen to the cells, found the Lourdes spring water contained an unusual amount of the trace mineral. This is also true of the much visited water fall up in the mountains of Japan which Dr. Asai tested and found to be well supplied with the trace mineral germanium.

Among other spas around the world, Sulphur Springs, Oklahoma, takes its place. Artesian wells provide the water that people from far and near come to drink for its minerals, especially sulphur. One wonders if the most therapeutic substance was natural oxygen forming in the water from the action of the artesian wells.

Oxygen is more abundant near the sea, a lake, a river and in a forest. Along with abundant negative ions in the air, breathing becomes truly healthful and healing. If we can't live near one of these ideal living areas, we need to take a vacation there. With clean, oxygenated air, natural cleansing food (mostly raw), and daily wholesome exercise, we can surely be rejuvenated.

Increasingly, hydrogen peroxide is finding its way into agriculture. Crops sprayed with it not only grow better, but are more resistant to insects and to plant diseases. Green house operators spray to keep down mold and mildew in their buildings and by so doing increase the growth and vigor of their plants because of the extra oxygenated air.

Numerous livestock people have installed an injector, an apparatus that continually puts proper concentrations of H_2O_2 into the animals watering system. Livestock growers spray with it for insects and drench sick animals, including calves, shoats and young chickens in it. Hydrogen peroxide is effective for spray cleaning and deodorizing, sheds, coops and barns.

They say their animals are healthier, the offspring larger and stronger, the meat firmer and less marbled with fat. To these growers, the added cost of installing and maintaining an H_2O_2 injector for extra oxygen is more than covered when they market their products.

Hydrogen peroxide is widely used in industry. Happily, food companies increasingly utilize it not only for cleanliness in processing plants and with food handling, but as an actual ingredient in processed food. Hydrogen peroxide extends the shelf life of many foods such as cheese and milk. It is used in wine making and a host of other products too numerous to mention here.

H_2O_2 leaves no residue. It causes no allergic reaction and assures purity in foods.

Products such as toothpaste, skin preparations, cosmetics, lotions for insect bites and rashes are coming onto the market. Little by little, hydrogen peroxide is being respected and utilized.

A physician in the 1930's said, "Oxygen is great stuff." Later another said, "Ozone will do for oxygen what oxygen can't do." A physicist, J. Hansler, for whom the Hansler Corporation, Germany, was named, solved the problem of reliable and precise application of ozone. From the results of his pioneering work, ozone therapy became widely and successfully used in medicine. His much copied ozone generator became the basis of modern medical ozone equipment.

What H_2O_2 Can Cure
And Is Curing

Chapter 8

What H$_2$O$_2$ Can Cure And Is Curing

Every day more people learn about naturally occurring hydrogen peroxide which in the body catalyses into oxygen and water. With its broad, curative, rejuvenating powers, it is the hope for all sufferers to be free of disease; the hope of all people to remain healthy and functioning for a long, energetic and fruitful lifetime.

Since all degenerative disease proliferates where cells do not get enough oxygen, it is logical to say that cells getting normal amounts of oxygen stay healthy. With optimal oxygen they cannot become diseased. With a scarcity of oxygen, cells change. They become anaerobic. They live with little or no oxygen supplied to them. That means they are not normal. They become weakened and then easy prey to disease.

The body of the patient suffering from degenerative disease is like a stagnant pool. In such a pool few plants or animals can survive. It is so oxygen poor, nothing will grow in the putrefaction but bad bacteria. To clean it up and have a pool of fresh water, we have to flush out the toxins, clear out the muck and debris, the putrefaction, the anaerobic microbes infesting it. Then with fresh, oxygenated water, we refill the pool and make it a clean environment for plants and animals alike. But to keep all such organisms alive and well, we must see that fresh, clean water continues to feed the pool.

Let's start with an example of a colon cancer patient whose body condition was not unlike the stagnant pool full of toxins, viruses, bacteria and other oxygen depleting debris. Although the cancer had metastasized to the bone, the doctor was able to remove the part most destroyed by the cancer, the ascending colon. He then **burned** the patient's body with radiation. Then **killed** vast numbers of living cells with **toxic chemotherapy**. The patient's immune system was all but ruined and any reserve of vitamins, minerals and enzymes he may have had were destroyed. His total health deteriorated so much he was given a few months to live.

In this nearly hopeless condition the patient's son took him to a clinic in Mexico that gets mostly last phase, terminal patients. After the usual laboratory tests, the patient started on I.V.'s of hydrogen peroxide and several nutrient supplements, pure water and fresh fruit juices. After the first day, he felt better. From then on he continued steadily to recover. In five months, feeling fine, he went back to work and has continued carrying on his business with no intention of retiring early.

A physician friend of mine, cautious of the powers of censorship within the orthodox medical community, treats his arthritic patients with H_2O_2, baths. He prescribes a few drops of food grade H_2O_2 in pure drinking water (See Appendix), an all natural diet and breathing exercises daily. He uses kinesiological muscle testing for determining their allergies. Besides advising them to avoid all foods that cause allergic or sensitive reactions, he prescribes a program of mostly raw foods. Lastly, he suggests a good, natural multi-mineral supplement and mega-doses of vitamin C. The pain and swelling not only soon go down, calcium deposits gradually dissolve.

There are countless documented, clinically recorded case histories of remission of degenerative disease using hydrogen peroxide therapies. A thick volume could be written about them. In this writing, we discuss only the tip of the iceberg. For more in depth studies, we suggest you go to the nearest university or public library to consult the excellent books and papers written in the last century on the subject.

Thousands of doctors in Germany, in Europe and in Scandinavia, well over one hundred in the United States and many in Mexico are using hydrogen peroxide and ozone successfully in the treatment of degenerative disease. Patients give testimony of remission from all kinds of disease. In Mexico, the University of Guadalajara Medical School, a recognized institution of high standards and investigative skills, is experimenting with bio-oxygenation therapies and reporting good results.

The great conqueror of disease turns out to be Oxygen in one or more of its many forms, either H_2O_2 or Ozone or **other available oxygen sources.** Even in the treatment of malaria, a parasite, not a bacterium, hydrogen peroxide is effective, according to experiments done in the Middlesex Hospital Medical School of London, England.

In our body there are cells that fight infestation, called granulocytes. They produce hydrogen peroxide. They are first to come to our defense when our bodies are invaded by every type of organism bacteria, viruses, yeast, parasites.

In summary, we list diseases in patients we personally know or have observed before and after bio-oxidative treatment. They are back working and give living witness to relief from the symptoms of degenerative disease:

AIDS	Heart Disease
Alzheimer's Disease	Hepatitis
Arthritis	Herpes Simplex
Asthma	Herpes Zoster
Cancer	Legionnaire's Disease
Candidiasis	Liver dysfunction
Chronic pulmonary disease	Lupus erythematosis
Chronic sinusitis	Multiple Sclerosis
Diabetes	Multiple, severe poisoning
Dizziness	Paralysis
Epstein Bar	Parkinson's Disease
Emphysema	Pesticide poisoning
Flu, pneumonia, bronchitis	Poor circulation
Gangrene	Syphilis

Truly, hydrogen peroxide and ozone are our agents of healing. No other chemical comes close. H_2O_2 is a part of all of our body's vital processes. Everything in life's function requires this compound—immunity, vitamin and mineral metabolism, fat, protein and carbohydrate metabolism.

Hydrogen peroxide and ozone are simple curatives. In proper concentrations, they cause great good with no harm. It is natural to the body. Could it be the miraculous cure mankind has always sought?

Note: The bitterness in herbs indicates the presence of oxygen. Quinine, extracted from a tree bark, is extremely bitter. It is an ancient, proven remedy for malaria. The Brazilian tree bark, Pau d'Arco, or teheebo, just inside the thin bark, has white crystals which contain oxygen. The bitter herbs of the Bible were effective, partly because of the oxygen containing, oxygen enhancing characteristic. Other herbs, recently proven effective against cancer, flu, arthritis, etc., are bitter, as is golden seal, chaparral and dandelion. Made into tea, elixir or liquid concentrate, their stored oxygen is released and readily enters the bloodstream for purification and rejuvenation when ingested.

Facts

And Fiction--
About Oxygenation

Chapter 9

Facts And Fiction About
Oxygenation

The more the subject of hydrogen peroxide (H_2O_2), and ozone (O_3) is pursued, the more exciting it gets. Investigative reporters and all kinds of interested researchers are turning up findings dating back to the early 1800's. The unraveling of the story of oxygen, (hydrogen peroxide and ozone therapy) reveals how it works in our body. We learn why we take on this or that disease and why the body does or does not heal. Most encouraging of all, we find out what can be done about disease quickly, easily and inexpensively.

It was discovered by Doctor Otto Warburg in the 1920's that cancer cells thrive in an *anaerobic* environment and when this environment is flooded with oxygen these same cancer cells die. Dr. Warburg is the only man to ever win the Nobel Prize twice in medicine and he was nominated for a third.

One of the discoveries made about H_2O_2 is that it is the first line of defense of our immune system. The immune system in normal function actually makes hydrogen peroxide. When the body is full of waste products and toxicity from eating processed, overcooked food, drinking chlorinated, fluoridated water, breathing polluted air, it is overworked. In trying to rid the system of waste and toxin, the body is weakened and can neither supply normal amounts of H_2O_2 to the cells nor cleanse out the debris. Insufficient oxygen in the system means low energy and fatigue. The body fails to manufacture healthy cells to create energy, clear out the "dirt" and at the same time keep all parts functioning. What may happen under all the stress is illness. It is especially true if the person does not exercise enough, has eaten oxygen deficient foods and is a shallow breather. All this can happen not only to the elderly but to the young and middle aged as well.

Our bodies can arrive at low levels of oxygen for a variety of reasons. They are so important, we list several of them here, for a second time.

1. The air we breathe, which should be at least 20% oxygen, may be as low as 10% in some cities. Oxygen in air bubbles trapped in ancient amber as well as core samples of ice taken from polar regions, have been found to be twice as high as in present day air.

2. Antibiotics, so much prescribed, kill the friendly bacteria that produce hydrogen peroxide in the intestines. This good bacteria also can synthesize B vitamins when it out numbers the bad bacteria. Considering the almost universal taking of antibiotics, is it any wonder that there is an equally universal deficiency of B vitamins in today's world?

3. Processing destroys the oxygen in foods.

4. Chlorine in drinking water destroys oxygen. Even in unchlorinated piped water, there will be a deficiency of oxygen from a lack of aeration in those sealed pipes.

5. Cooking (heating) fruits and vegetables and roasting nuts and seeds drives out oxygen.

6. Not only are hydrogenated and processed foods oxygen poor, they add a lot of debris (indigestible food particles) that overtax the already overworked circulation system. It requires time and effort for the body to haul this debris around in the bloodstream, leaving less time and energy for the body to take in oxygen. The result is oxygen deficiency.

How important is oxygen? Our bodies need between 6 and 8 pounds of oxygen a day. That's nearly twice the required combined weight of food (4 pounds) and water (2 pounds). We cannot deny the utter importance of oxygen.

In the Journal of the American Medical Association's May, 1974 issue, appeared an article written by George B. Hart, M.D. The article was about three patients critically ill with hypoxia (oxygen deficiency) who refused blood transfusions because of their beliefs. All were given hyperbaric oxygen treatments with ensuing remission of symptoms. Although all three had insufficient blood volume, they had blood well saturated with life and health giving oxygen. All recovered.

In the 1969 issue of the New England Journal of Medicine, appeared a report of Dr. Nair on senile patients. They suffered from chronic vertigo (dizziness) and mental sluggishness. After receiving hyperbaric oxygen therapy, they all improved.

Hyperbaric oxygen treatment has helped many patients with osteomyelitis. Doctors administered oxygen under high pressure (OHP). Some researchers concluded that both the OHP and the stimulated immune system were involved in bringing about the remission of the disease.

Before retiring each night, our custom is to take a ten minute dip in the hot tub treated with H_2O_2. Not only is our tiredness soon gone, but a feeling of peace and wellness comes over us. Besides these personal benefits, the pool stays fresh and clean for months instead of weeks. (If we are unusually tired or threatened with a cold or flu, we add more than our usual two cups of 35% hydrogen peroxide).

The process of aging has been explained as follows: As we grow older, our bodies take in less and less oxygen unless we do something to correct that process. Where there is oxygen deficiency, the body does not assimilate vitamin C well, which means a weakening of collagen, the "glue" that hold the cells together. Tissues become flabby, veins and arteries harden, and the way is prepared for brain deterioration and stroke. Oxygen therapy is turning this around for some.

Intoxication from alcohol abuse comes about because the brain has been robbed of oxygen. By the reverse action, extra oxygen in the bloodstream seems to restore mental action and lessen craving for alcohol. The same seems to hold true in the case of the overuse of drugs. We've heard that putting an intoxicated person in a bathtub half full of water oxygenated with seven to ten pints of 3% hydrogen peroxide will restore him/her to normal in a matter of minutes without a hangover. Since we have not been called upon to meet such an emergency, we cannot vouch for the effectiveness of the treatment. We do feel, however, it is well worth the try. It's inexpensive and harmless.

According to scientists, extra oxygen along with a cleansing diet can return balance to the body. It can also help remove cravings that lead to addictions such as alcohol, nicotine, food, drugs, and caffeine.

In 1951, the German Physicist Dr. Johanna Budwig began publishing papers on how oxygen is taken into the red blood cells of the lungs, and carbon dioxide given off. According to her, it is the complicated process of the oxidation enhancing fatty acids getting the oxygen into the cells. The way to bring this about, she reported, was to eat *essential* polyunsaturated fatty acids. The best source was the oil in flaxseed, with carotene a close second. For nearly forty years she worked at informing the world about the efficacy of flaxseed oil and the oxygen destruction of hydrogenated oils.

Have you ever wondered what is meant by *hydrogenated fats and oils?* It means hydrogen, a light, highly inflammable, toxic gas, is bubbled through oil to make it solid (margarine) thus severely distorting the molecules themselves. A small amount of the gas, along with solvents, is put through vegetable oils to make them clear, tasteless, colorless, odorless and free of sediment. Such oils turn out to be not only devoid of nutrition, but harmful as well. It shows up as sticky plaque on the walls of the blood vessels. Cholesterol then clings to this sticky plaque.

According to Dr. Budwig and Urdo Erasmus, research investigators of the properties of flax seed, the oil extracted therefrom is particularly effective for supplying essential nutrients. Erasmus' findings seem to coincide with and verify Dr. Budwig's conclusion that the *electron-rich* fats in flaxseed, in harmony with sunlight wavelengths, enhance and in fact control the very life process of the body. Therefore, if we eat hydrogenated (nutrition destroyed) oils or fried foods, we deplete our body's oxygen and undermine our health.

A little stressed item in our daily living indirectly involving oxygen is extremely important. The chewing (masticating) of food. Without breaking down food particles to a smooth cream, there cannot be truly good digestion. Without optimal digestion, there cannot be normal absorption and assimilation of nutrients by the cells. Without sufficient absorption and assimilation, there cannot be good health. Without truly good health, our body does not take in enough oxygen and eventually falls prey to disease. With a lack of this one nutrient, oxygen, cells mutate and we have, once again, the beginning of degenerative disease.

Our nephew, a medical researcher, said after discussing oxygen with us, "Why didn't I think of it before? In the lab, when we want cells to mutate, we diminish the oxygen. Those mutated cells continue to live in the degenerative state only with little or no oxygen. They become anaerobic."

Let us keep remembering: cancer cells are anaerobic. Dr. F. M. Eugene Blass, in 1929 wrote, "*Oxidation is the source of life and health. Impaired oxidation means disease. Cessation of oxidation is death.*"

THE UNMEDICAL MIRACLE—Oxygen

Ozone And
Hydrogen Peroxide

In The World Of
Medcal Research

Chapter 10

Ozone And Hydrogen Peroxide In The World Of Medical Research

Happily, there is much going on in the field of hydrogen peroxide and ozone research. Many of the investigations are verifying the positive claims for hydrogen peroxide and ozone, far more than they did a century past. Moreover, we are seeing the emergence of innovative ways of using them for health and disease remission.

One of the oldest references to the therapeutic use of hydrogen peroxide we found in an old book about cures. Back in 1746 hydrogen peroxide and bicarbonate of soda were advocated for the treatment of pus pockets around teeth. After the combination was rubbed into the gums, a dentist cleaned out the dead tissue and the patient continued further applications at home until the mouth was free of infection.

Some years ago before we got off processed food and a cooked diet, one of us was going through a general breakdown in health. The dentist said he would have to surgically trim away the diseased tissue of the gums next to the teeth. To us, the treatment sounded drastic. No way was this butchery acceptable. We chose to use old fashioned hydrogen peroxide along with newer vitamin C. Soon there was no more bleeding, pus or pain. Twenty years later and with an all natural, mostly raw diet, the gums are as healthy as, to quote our dentist, "A seventeen year old's."

Reports come into IOMA and the International Ozone Association from around the world of doctors using ozone for the successful treatment of almost all known degenerative disease, the likes of which include cancer and HIV infections. Repeated applications destroy diseased cells without harming healthy cells. What happens is a weakening of the enzymatic coating of the diseased cells on contact with the ozone. The extra oxygen from the ozone helps the natural immune system and its cells to attack and invade the virus cells. These virus cells are really parasites, unable to reproduce themselves on their own.

Hepatitis responds to ozone therapy by disappearing in days, as does herpes zoster and herpes simplex.

The pain of the accompanying neuritis, neuralgic inflammation ceases in a few more days.

Ozone also dates back to the eighteenth century. Martinus Van Marum in 1785 made notes on an oxidizing agent and its pungent odor, although ozone was not actually identified until 1840 when C.F. Schönbein named it *ozone,* meaning, in Greek, odorant.

More work was done with ozone in Germany in the latter part of the nineteenth century. From the discovery that ozone can destroy toxic and foul smelling bacteria, came its first use of purifying drinking water in 1901, in the city of Weisbaden, Germany.

From then until now many cities in Europe and elsewhere in the world have used and are using ozone as a primary source of disinfection to purify their drinking water. Some specific ones are Marseille, Brussels, Moscow, Zurich, and Singapore as well as Los Angeles, (the largest in the U.S.) San Francisco, 10 other cities in the S.F. Bay Area and several more cities across the U.S. with others following.

What a pity U.S. cities have listened to profit minded industry and continue to pour poisons—chlorine and fluoride—into our drinking water. Both subtly destroy health. Is it any wonder that among the developed countries of the world, we have the highest per capita occurrence, for example, of cancer, heart disease and AIDS? Ozone or hydrogen peroxide treated water, on the contrary, restore health and help prevent disease.

The author quotes the article of Sweet, Kao et.al. *Science* 1980 as saying, "Ozone selectively inhibited the growth of human cancer cells." Since it kills viruses, bacteria, and fungi, isn't it logical for us to support further research today on a subject of so much interest? It could eliminate the doubt and ignorance that keeps one of the greatest medical benefits from general practice in a world where almost everyone has a problem it could help.

Unfortunately, the status of ozone has been so incompletely reported that the public has been led to believe it is toxic and harmful. A host of documented examples of ozone therapy has come into existence without anyone correlating and arranging it for clear understanding.

We need to gather abundant information on some of it's more repeatable and important uses. It might lift this natural, highly curative substance out of the mire of misunderstanding, controversy and false, incorrect propaganda it tragically has fallen into. In the 1940's, France declared ozone the number one treatment for cancer.

Hydrogen peroxide is a colorless, odorless liquid. It is completely soluble in water. We usually think of the three percent solution sold by the drugstore. It's commonly known uses are (1) as a bleach; (2) as an antiseptic and disinfectant; (3) as a deodorant; (4) as an oxidizing agent, and (5) as an oxidizer in small rocket motors.

In the latter half of the 1800's, three percent hydrogen peroxide was determined to be the correct strength for maximum bactericidal application without harm to the skin. After that it began to be used quite generally among physicians, especially during and after the Civil War.

Hydrogen peroxide should certainly be thought of much more than as a mouth wash and topical disinfectant. It has been called the weapon of our killer cells, the polymorphonuclear leukocytes. What happens is the cells mix oxygen and water, making hydrogen peroxide. This biological activity, called the *respiratory burst,* first identifies the enemy then destroys it. Hydrogen Peroxide to the rescue in our immune system!

This action is so important we need to restate it for clarity: first, the white cells mix oxygen and water. The resulting respiratory burst is suddenly formed hydrogen peroxide which surrounds the invading bacteria and oxidizes it. Amazing! Hydrogen peroxide is not just a disinfectant for cut fingers. It is one of our most important body defenses.

Other cells besides leukocytes, called granulocytes, also produce H_2O_2, a top fighter of all kinds of invading organisms. These cells can destroy viruses, yeast and parasites as well as bacteria. "No other chemical compound comes even close to H_2O_2 in its importance to life on this earth, except that of ozone. H_2O_2 and ozone are involved in all of life's vital processes: protein, carbohydrate and fat metabolism, vitamin and mineral metabolism, immunity and anything else involving life's functions."

According to the reports of several researchers into the hydrogen peroxide story, there are well over six thousand articles in science publications since 1920. Those of us who have delved into the history, authenticity and effectiveness of H_2O_2 are aware of many articles in the scientific literature dating back to its discovery in the 1700's. How incredible it is that in the past seventy years this wealth of information on reported cures and clinical evidence has been almost completely ignored in today's medical practice.

Some one-liner's of information about hydrogen peroxide:

H_2O_2 action is similar to insulin—it aids the transport of sugar through the system.

After the infusion of hydrogen peroxide in therapy, venous blood is the bright, clean red of arterial blood which carries more oxygen than venous blood.

Vitamin C in its reaction to inflammation appears to offer benefits through the making of hydrogen peroxide.

By generating hydrogen peroxide, vitamin C protects against infections.

It appears at this time that hydrogen peroxide may be as vital, or more, as thyroid for the generation of heat. With co-enzyme Q10, H_2O_2, brings about a warming of the cells, essential for life.

Incidentally, the therapeutic effect of hydrogen peroxide given in the vein is equal to that given the hyperbaric way and at a fraction of the cost.

Some twenty five years ago, a team of physicians of the Baylor University Medical Center found that if the oxygen supply to the tissues was maximal, those tissues were more sensitive to radiation therapy. Cancer cells don't like oxygen (H_2O_2 or ozone). And they don't like X-rays. The two forces working together, physicians found, had a destructive effect on the cancer cells.

The Baylor physicians also found that H_2O_2 infusion into the blood vessel was quadruple that of hyperbaric oxygen. Furthermore, it had no side effects whatsoever. The same could not be said of hyperbaric oxygen. Not only is there danger of too much pressure, the cost of it is many times greater than intravenous H_2O_2. Another startling fact they discovered was that hydrogen peroxide dripped into arteries of severely afflicted arteriosclerosis patients cleaned those vessels of plaque (lipid) buildup. What a medical achievement, and how simple and inexpensive, yet no one listened or followed the practice. (Later follow-up studies and investigation showed the improvement *lasted*.)

As the story of H_2O_2 and ozone unfolds, we see a great turn-around in the use of medicines from synthetic drugs (poisoning), unnatural surgery (butchery) and radiation (burning) to the natural therapies GOD intended.

The Suppression Of Bio-Oxidative Treatment In The United States

Chapter 11

The Suppression Of Bio-Oxidative Treatment In The United States

A question constantly arises to haunt us all. Why have oxygenation therapies been suppressed? With people throughout the world suffering from problems and diseases that can be helped by hydrogen peroxide and/or ozone, what a tragedy we've all been denied this relief!

At this writing, statistical studies of the rising incidence of cancer reveal that it now afflicts over fifty percent of the population in the United States. The prevalence of skin cancer nearly matches that of terminal cancer. From first diagnosis of terminal cancer through surgery, chemotherapy and/or radiation treatment, costs run from $45,000 to $60,000 dollars. After all of that invasive treatment, the patient's body is so damaged and weakened, he/she has an average life expectancy of three years.

In contrast, bio-oxidative therapy of hydrogen peroxide or ozone, *natural therapies,* supplements, and a clean, all natural mostly raw food diet may cost a few hundred to a few thousand dollars. During the treatment, the patient's general health is built up and restored instead of torn down and destroyed.

A Dr. William F. Koch developed what has become known as "The Koch Treatment" for some of the most prevalent diseases of our times, cancer being one of the first treated in 1918. The basis of Dr. Koch's science is:

The chemistry of the *natural immunity* of the body is able to destroy the toxicity of germs.

When the body is invaded by toxic bacteria that poisons the system, the mechanism of **oxidation** must burn off the poisons or the person becomes ill.

The less able the system is to oxidize the toxins the weaker the person becomes. When the **oxidation** process fails, the result is death.

Dr. Koch developed synthetic anti-toxins which act as a catalyst to help the body rebuild its oxidation mechanism to the point where it can destroy these toxins.

Born before the turn of the century, Dr. Koch practiced in Detroit, MI from before the early 1920's until he chose to leave the US. in the 60's.

Those medically effective results threatened the controlled status quo of the present dark ages in science which resulted in continual professional and government harassment of his work.

Throughout his career there were astounding results credited to this treatment of his, from doctors to veterinarians who found the treatment to be so effective on cattle diseases.

Unfortunately, the pressure became too great for Dr. Koch to practice in the U.S. and he left the country in the 1960's to continue his work in Brazil. He consistently maintained unqualified success in his work until his death under suspicious circumstances.

It has been established to the satisfaction of many practicing physicians that most of the degenerative diseases can be conquered with bio-oxidative treatment at a small fraction of the cost of conventional therapies.

The medical establishment and pharmaceutical companies, the hospitals, laboratories and clinics would crumble if the present status quo were to change. With ninety plus percent of the diseases eradicated by a simple, non-prescription chemical that is harmless in proper levels of concentration and application, the whole structure would collapse.

Can you see all the **sick** care industry deliberately decimating their world of an established, highly lucrative, technical, automated medical monopoly? Not likely!

The economics of the vast situation is not the only reason for suppression of the therapy. Pride plays a great part. It's a shattering experience, a near fatal blow to realize something has made obsolete much of what has been learned through many years of medical practice. It's like yanking the rug out from under them. It is difficult to endure what is viewed as the humiliation of a fall.

In all due respect to doctors and the whole sick care support structure, we ask a question: Would any of us be willing enough to give up such an affluent livelihood for the sake of healing and alleviating the ills of humanity? It's a noble cause, but how many heroes are there among us?

The structure of the combined big medical, pharmaceutical and government interest has such intertwining support it is all but indomitable. Only the concerted, persistent, determined effort of the public will change it. The F.D.A. (Food and Drug Administration), the A.M.A. (American Medical Association), the Pharmaceuticals and the American Cancer Society are large and powerful. The F.D.A. is pressured by industry and too often yields to their money making demands. Food and drug companies push to get new profit yielding products approved for sale. The pharmaceuticals promote drugs, a highly profitable business. Doctors, trained in disease and symptom treatment for quick relief instead of finding and treating causes, are of course drug oriented. The pharmaceutical industry pays for the publication of the journal of the American Medical Association. Power attracts power. The American Cancer Society, funded mainly by the Federal Government, is reluctant to admit a cancer cure that would end their self-perpetuating, multi-billion dollar existence.

The situation is comfortable for many thousands of researchers, doctors, technicians and the vast portion of support employees in offices, laboratories and maintenance departments. They are not arbitrarily going to change. Can you imagine these mammoth entities making public a cure for cancer, explaining its low cost, the painless recovery, the beneficial effects it has on a patient's general health, the prevention of disease it can assure? Do you visualize the media voluntarily explaining over and over all of this to the general public until *everyone* understands? The pharmaceuticals, the A.C.S. and the F.D.A. are not about to recognize bio-oxidative treatment of disease. It is a threat to the existence they now enjoy. The news media, with its known bias, will in most cases not even print the stories of curative, health giving and preventive results of bio-oxidative therapy.

It is up to each one of us, the people, to take the responsibility for our own health. We must find out all we can about H_2O_2 and O_3, what is going on in the fields of research and treatment, then spread the news. A good place to start is to write to our county, state, and federal representatives. We can tell them our views on the use of toxic chlorine and fluoride in the drinking water and inform them of the statistics that show the increasing incidence of degenerative disease in our area. Then we must let them know what can be done if we find out *they* were the ones who knew about the oxygen therapies for AIDS and cancer remission but made no effort to let us, their constituents, know about it.

We each need to help get the word out to all such public servants as health officials, policemen, teachers, prison case workers, street people, social workers and missionaries. It is urgent they learn that superoxygenation can protect them from HIV infection.

A couple we know have become so dedicated to getting the "word" out to others, they hand out copies of oxygen information wherever they go. That is many places in the United States of America. It is their "calling." They are enjoying meeting countless people vitally interested in helping themselves and others to better physical health and mental function. This couple anticipates and enjoys each day of their now healthy lives.

Share this good news with any and all people about what H_2O_2 and the other oxygen therapies can do for the health problems we face today, big and small, major and minor. It seems to relieve or eliminate everything from athlete's foot and warts to psoriasis and cancer. The slogan could well be: optimal oxygen, optimal health; minimum oxygen, minimum health.

Most certainly, let's help others to stop thinking that heart disease, cancer, emphysema, multiple sclerosis, and so on, are pronouncements of death.

Recently friends whom we hadn't seen for some time came by. They looked exceptionally well and were enjoying *good spirits* as they described their positive outlook and great energy. They had quite a story to tell which they related with the enthusiasm that accompanies experiences with happy endings.

Jim started with flashing a broad smile revealing his beautiful new teeth. "For several years I had problems with my gums and losing my teeth. Just last summer I finally conquered the problem. Periodontal surgeons, hygienists, our family dentist and a dental surgeon all had their try at me. My mouth simply would not heal. Then I learned to use hydrogen peroxide as a mouth wash. That ended all my gum problems. But in the midst of it all, Susanne got sick. Suffering aches and pains doctors couldn't explain, she came down with pneumonia. That was in August a year ago. Two antibiotic prescriptions and ten days later her temperature was back to normal. We were so thankful it had all ended." Jim hesitated, looking at his wife.

"But it hadn't," she continued. "In September, an intense pain started in my thigh then extended clear down to my ankle. It turned out to be phlebitis of the deep blood vessels. The doctor gave me Prednisone and Tylenol. I couldn't take aspirin because of the Cumarin I was taking. The pain got better and the doctor gradually lowered the dose. Then in November, I began having a severe lung problem. The biopsy showed another type of inflammation. For several weeks I breathed oxygen from a tank. After a couple of weeks I was no better and the oxygen was bothering my throat, making me hoarse. The doctors wanted to do an operation for a bigger biopsy. They weren't satisfied with the first one. They thought I had cancer. I didn't think so. My color wasn't gray-white. Jim and I both felt I'd be much better in our winter quarters in Mexico. After we got there I started running a temperature, then came down with bronchitis. Jim met two people who have wonderful health. Both overcame all sorts of major life threatening illnesses. They did it with oxygen supplementation and a nearly all raw, natural diet. After reading some of their literature, we got off all processed and junk foods and drinks. We did take a few supplements; vitamin C and E, and a natural B vitamin supplement. And I took hydrogen peroxide in my drinking water."

"I soon started taking it too," Jim said. "We got the food grade thirty-five percent solution and started with the minimum dose and increasing it a little bit at a time. Susanne was not nauseated but she didn't like the taste. It didn't bother me at all. We both began to feel better in two or three weeks. We've been taking it eleven months now. I haven't had an asthma attack for five months. And my arthritis doesn't pain me anymore."

"We both have good energy," Susanne said. "It's wonderful. The candida a doctor found I had when we returned home is gone. My lungs feel good, the phlebitis is no more and my energy is just fine. Jim has not had a cold or the flu and I haven't had bronchitis or phlebitis or pneumonia."

Jim had the last word. "We only do two things different. Susanne fixes mostly vegetarian foods and I see to it that we get our H_2O_2 daily."

THE UNMEDICAL MIRACLE—Oxygen

The Unmedical Miracle Triplets—

 Oxygen

 Food

 Water

Chapter 12

The UnMedical Miracle Triplets—
Oxygen, Food And Water

The broad spectrum of services oxygen can render our bodies, minds and environment is enormous. However, oxygen isn't everything. It cannot do it all. Close to the importance of oxygen are food and water. Without them our oxygen would run out of anything to service.

Of course we all make a stab at seeing that we have fresh water to drink. But do we succeed, really? Do we object to fluoride, a proven carcinogenic additive with the unproven service of, "keeping down cavities in the teeth?" Do we question the amount of chlorine, which is excessive, and the toxic, carcinogenic chemical itself contaminating the water and zapping the vitamins from our bodies? Both fluoride and chlorine destroy oxygen in the water. Yet with super oxygenation, water can be purified, freshened and freed from harsh and unpleasant tastes while improving and sustaining our health. In contrast, fluoride and chlorine subtly tear it down. It's yet another example of industry overprofiting from a surplus by-product of manufacturing, then through constant propaganda, passing it off on a gullible, unsuspecting public. We could do well to take a tip from our European neighbors who mostly purify their drinking water and pools with ozone or hydrogen peroxide. Since water is a means through which we get more health giving oxygen, we need to provide oxygenated fresh water for drinking, bathing and swimming, in that order.

The discussion about food has been reserved for the last because it can be the most pleasant. And since, in our food, there is a way for us to get a lot of oxygen for our bodies, it is doubly a joy to anticipate.

No greater pleasure delights us than a bowl full of beautiful, colorful, fresh, shiny fruits or vegetables. What a tragedy that mankind has fallen into the habit of killing them by heat.

There is an appropriate but sad analogy to be made that emphasizes the difference between dead food and live food. Here it is. In order to transport a body from the deathbed to the hearse, it takes from two to four carriers. By the same token, dead food cells killed from cooking or processing must be transported by carriers in the digestive tract to the bloodstream to nourish the body. The dead food is dead weight. Live foods carry their own weight. The energy for dead food transport, like a car burning unclean fuel, leaves residues and debris in the tissues that are toxins. Toxins help cause degenerative disease. As a live, healthy body provides energy for transport, so do living foods provide for their transport through digestion and assimilation.

There is every reason for eating food fresh from the garden or orchard and none for cooking them. First, cooking destroys from 30 to 85 percent of the nutrition. Enzymes are completely destroyed. Our health is about as good as the supply of enzymes provided for our digestion. Vitamin C is mostly destroyed as are the B vitamins, especially B_6. The fat soluble vitamins A, D, E and K can survive boiling temperature of 212 degrees. They are, however, destroyed in the high temperatures of baking, broiling, roasting and frying, along with the essential oils linolenic and linoleic acid. Minerals are poured off in the cooking liquids, and the oxygen is mostly destroyed.

Note: Some people cannot digest raw foods. Their weakened digestive system cannot break down the cells of raw fruits, vegetables, nuts, seeds and sprouts. In that case, cells need to be broken down completely. This can be done by freezing, dehydrating, blending, or chewing everything, even bananas, avocado and milk, at least 50 times a bite.

We pay a lot for fresh foods, bring them home, spend hours killing them by baking, boiling or microwaving them, destroy most of their nutrients and by doing so add some indigestible debris to our bodies. As though that were not enough harm, we often over eat as well. Overeating, according to many physicians, is a major cause of degenerative disease.

Most of us moan over the high cost of food. What we had better complain about is the high cost of illness, usually brought on by the way we prepare our foods and the amount we consume. When we eat raw foods we are not tempted to overeat. They are bulky without being heavy. They fill without making us feel stuffed and uncomfortable. The full complement of nutrients in living foods keeps the body healthy and the appetite normal. Raw foods help us overcome a faulty appetite and food addiction. It is *slow* murder and suicide.

When people hear or read about the advisability of an all natural, nearly all raw way of eating, they think *vegetarian* and that means to them living on salads. No way are they going to do that. I don't blame them. I couldn't either, and didn't. Living vegetables, fruits, nuts and seeds can be made into vegetable casseroles, soups, nut/seed loaves, patties, desserts and snack foods, dips and treats.

For some, a vegetarian life mode may not be necessary for optimal health. There are those who may choose to be ovo-lacto vegetarian (eggs-milk products), or just ovo or lacto. The majority of people during early childhood normally lose the body enzyme, lactase, for digesting lactose in milk products. Some continue through life able to metabolize lactose. Most people can eat eggs if they are soft boiled or soft poached. They can also digest butter, which is a good food. Butter is a balance between hard fat and polyunsaturated fat. Without some hard fat, we become more cancer prone. Margarine, with its artificial color and flavor, is hydrogenated to make it hard. It is all bad. So eat natural butter, *but in moderation.*

Many people may never be convinced fish and chicken are anything but the very best of foods for strength, stamina, energy and a good immune system. However, not only is sea water generally polluted, but also most fresh water, making the catch at risk for causing disease. As time goes on, some commercial poultrymen are adopting methods of growing that will produce a cancer free liver in the bird. If you must eat chicken find out if it has been grown in a healthy environment.

The chance of toxic, diseased foods of both animal and plant sources is too real for comfort. Hepatitis alone has quadrupled in the last decade. Liver diseases are on a rapid rise. Scientists suspect polluted waters contaminating the sea food as being the main cause.

The vegetarian does not have that worry about the extra cost of flesh foods. He does, however, need to address the problem of food sprays and dips.

There are several ways of at least partially neutralizing contaminants on fruits and vegetables. Place one heaping tablespoon of baking soda per gallon of water for soaking fresh fruits and vegetables for a few minutes after they've been washed.

Then after shaking off the water, rinse in a half gallon of water to which one quarter cup of vinegar has been added and soak a few minutes. In this way, whether the chemical on the fresh food is alkaline or acidic, the toxin will have been mostly neutralized. Or soak fruits and vegetables 20-30 minutes in hydrogen peroxide water. (See Appendix)

Everyone should do all that is possible to find naturally grown fruits and vegetables where compost and organic fertilizers are used instead of incomplete commercial fertilizers. Sprays, dips, pesticides and herbicides should cause the living food eater grave concern. Fortunately, each year sees more sources of organically grown produce available. This includes nuts, seeds and grains.

Ideally, we should all have a garden where we could grow the food, prepare it soon after harvesting and serve it immediately. The maximum nutrition is still there to nourish us. Our body thanks us with optimal performance. We can't all have a garden but we can all germinate seeds, nuts and grains. Not only does germinating (budding) yield the greatest concentration and the highest quality of food, it is the very least expensive. The greatest part for the career person who is struggling with budgets of time and money, is that of budding and sprouting. They require but minutes a day to produce. Meal preparation is simple and quick. Cleanup afterwards is a breeze with no grease, no plugged drain, no scrubbing.

For us, being thoroughly human and having a good appetite, the basis for much of our enthusiasm is the beautiful, brightly colored appearance of natural living foods. Of course the endless gourmet tastes give us eating excitement at each meal. Everything is so savory and flavorful, we live on special treats in infinite variety. Our friends who used to gently ridicule and make jokes about our *odd ball foods* are coming around to the all natural way of eating.

They are buying less and less processed foods and experiencing health improvement.

In summary, let us reiterate that bio-oxidative therapies are great. They are effective against disease and help to boost a low immune system. They should be sought after and investigated by every responsible adult interested in his/her health, recovery and prevention of disease. However, they can't do everything. Food, water, exercise and the right spirit *must* all be addressed. It takes a whole program of eating, drinking, exercising, resting, thinking and believing to result in a whole person, well functioning in body, mind and spirit.

Afterward

The information that has been provided here in this book is for the education of the public. It is a serious attempt to help people to recognize there is a way out of seemingly hopeless situations. The miracle of oxygen is for your benefit, for your upliftment.

Due to constraints above and beyond us, we are unable to include all the information available on oxygen in this book. There are products and therapies not touched upon or only mentioned in brief. These are by no means of any less importance to the individual than those already mentioned. Some products and services are more readily available in certain areas than others. It is for this reason that all of the possible avenues be explored so that the benefits of this wonderful substance can be made known and utilized by each and everyone of us who may need it.

Hydrogen peroxide and ozone are only two examples of oxygen in its many forms. However, there are still other forms that will provide substantial amounts of oxygen to the body. The use of stabilized oxygen, a product where oxygen is made stable in solution and added to water to increase oxygen intake by the individual, is an effective way to gain increased oxygen. The apparent drawback to this method is the high cost. Another example of products that enhance oxygen intake is mineral oxides. There are several of these products on the market, each claiming to provide oxygen to the system. Basically it is oxygen or ozone that is bonded to a mineral compound by a process that is either patented or held in a family trust. The positive action of this oxygen on the system makes it a highly effective natural purifier. These preparations must be introduced into the digestive tract, the most effective way being by bonding it (oxygen) to other substances such as minerals or water. Magnesium and Calcium are two of the minerals used for this purpose. Depending on the product and process used, there are varying amounts of oxygen that can be released into the body. These products are non-toxic and not habit forming.

Therefore, it is very important for all of you who read this book to look at and explore all of the resources available. You must be the ones to make the choices that will lead to more informed and healthy options for your health care.

Appendix

Appendix

Uses Of Hydrogen Peroxide Of Appropriate Concentrations

*(**Note:** 35% hydrogen peroxide is highly concentrated and extremely strong. Keep out of the reach of children. If it is spilled on the skin, wash immediately in cold water. Do not allow it to touch the eyes. If this happens, wash and rinse thoroughly with cold water.)*

Three percent hydrogen peroxide is the acceptable concentration for personal or household use. It is the strength sold in drug stores and supermarkets.

To make 3% H_2O_2, mix one ounce of 35% food grade to 11 ounces of distilled water (preferably) or filtered water.

Store 35% H_2O_2 in the freezer. Out of refrigeration, it will lose strength (potency) at the rate of approximately one percent a month.

Personal Uses For H202

Athlete's Foot: Soak feet 10 to 20 minutes each night in 3% H_2O_2 until condition is in remission.

Bath: To one bathtub half full of water, add one half cup 35% H_2O_2 (or one to five pints of 3% H_2O_2), one half cup rock salt, one half cup baking soda or Epsom Salts and soak 20 to 30 minutes.

Colonic: Mix one half to one pint 3% H_2O_2 to five gallons lukewarm water. (Never use more than one pint.)

Douche: Add five to six tablespoons 3% H_2O_2 to one quart distilled water.

Enema: Mix six tablespoons (maximum) 3% H_2O_2 to one quart distilled water.

Eye Wash: Use oxygenated drinking water in eye cup with pinch of sea salt (the saltiness of tears) dissolved in it before retiring. For best eye therapy, instead of salt, dissolve one eighth teaspoon of sodium ascorbate (vitamin C). This puts vitamin C where it is most needed. (The eyes along with the adrenals, need higher amounts of vitamin C than other organs in the body. Note: The solution should be the saltiness of tears.

Facial: For rejuvenation and freshening after washing, saturate a cotton wad with 3% H_2O_2 and gently rub on face and neck.

Foot relaxer: Add one to two ounces 3% H_2O_2 to one gallon of hot water and soak one half to one hour.

Mouthwash: On arising rinse mouth with water then gargle and wash mouth with 3% H_2O_2, swishing for one half to one minute. (Note: A dash of chlorophyll adds flavor and effectiveness.) Helps prevent colds.

Nasal Spray: 1 tablespoon of 3% H_2O_2 added to 1 cup of pure water. Spray into nasal passages to relieve congestion.

Stabilized oxygen drops: There are several companies that make stabilized oxygen drops for putting in drinking water. They are more expensive than hydrogen peroxide but do not cause nausea.

Pets: Add one ounce 3% H_2O_2 to one quart drinking water.

Rejuvenation: To one half bath tub of very warm water, add one and one half to two cups of 3% H_2O_2 and soak one hour or more. Good for immune system.

Shower: (Note: *Soap used in the shower removes the protective, acid mantle on the skin.*) Spray after showering, with 3% H_2O_2 to restore the natural acid mantle of the skin.

Toothpaste: Make a paste of baking soda and H_2O_2 and store in tightly sealed container. Or dip brush in 3% H_2O_2 and brush teeth.

Drink: One ounce of 35% food grade H_2O_2 in one gallon purified water, or filtered water. Also, one to ten or more drops of 35% food grade H_2O_2 in purified water. Many people like to drink a glass of oxygenated water three to six times a day or more.

Vaporizer: One ounce of 35% H_2O_2 per gallon of purified water in a vaporizer improves nighttime breathing and helps clear sinus and bronchial congestion.

Household Use Of Hydrogen Peroxide

Crop Spray: Many farmers are increasing crop yields by spraying with a dilute H_2O_2 water mixture. For each acre add 5 to 16 ounces of 35% Hydrogen Peroxide to 20 gallons of water.

Dishwasher: Add two to three ounces of 3% H_2O_2 to regular wash for dishes. Add the same for washing dishes in sink.

Deodorant: (Body) Saturate cotton wad with 3% H_2O_2 and rub on under arms.

Formaldehyde detox: The interiors of houses, closets, cabinets and bookcases, etc., made with particle board can be somewhat detoxified by spraying with a 3% solution of H_2O_2 on all exposed particle board surfaces several times a year for a few years.

Green Salad: For leftover salad, spray with solution of one tablespoon 3% H_2O_2 in 1/2 cup pure water. Drain and cover then refrigerate.

House and Garden Plants (for Growth): To one quart water add one ounce 3% H_2O_2 (or add to one quart water, 16 drops of 35% H_2O_2.) Mist and/or water plants frequently.

Household Spray for Freshener: In center of rooms spray 3% H_2O_2.

Humidifiers: Mix one pint 3% H_2O_2 in one gallon water and use in these apparatuses.

Insect Spray: In one gallon water stir eight ounces (one cup) refined white sugar and five to eight ounces 3% H_2O_2.

Kitchen Cleanser, Freshener, Disinfectant: Keep bottle of 3% H_2O_2 in refrigerator. Spray walls, underneath stove vent cover, room comers. Generously spray counter top and wipe with clean cloth.

Laundry: Instead of bleach, add six ounces of 3% H_2O_2 to small load of laundry; eight ounces to large load.

Marinade: In glass, stainless steel or ceramic casserole (never aluminum), place meat, poultry or fish and cover with 3% H_2O_2. Cover loosely and store in refrigerator one half to one hour. Rinse well then cook.

Mold: Spray or wash well with 3% H_2O_2, floors, corners, walls and ceilings; backs and underside of furniture; all around windows. Wipe dry with cloth if too damp.

(Note: Molds and mildews are a major cause of allergies, colds, bronchial and flu sensitivities; general malaise, breathing problems and low energy.)

Vegetable Soak: To a sinkful of cold water, add one half to one cup H_2O_2, and soak leafy vegetables 15 to 20 minutes. Soak thick skinned vegetables as zucchini, cucumbers, tomatoes, 25 to 30 minutes.

Glossary

Aerobic - living and growing in the presence of oxygen.

Anaerobic - living or active in the absence of free oxygen.

Antioxidant - a substance that opposes oxidation or inhibits a reaction promoted by oxygen. Enhances the body's utilization of oxygen. Helps to destroy excessive free radicals in the body.

Candida Albicans - a yeast over-growing the friendly flora of the intestines especially after the taking of antibiotics. It can infest all cavities as mouth, throat, bronchial tubes, ear canal, vagina, etc. It may eventually even become systemic (invading the blood stream and going to all parts of the body).

Candidiasis - The inflammation of candida albicans.

Catalase - An enzyme in the blood and tissues that catalyzes the decomposition of hydrogen peroxide into water and oxygen.

CO-Q10 (Co-enzyme Q10) - an energizing enzyme useful in regulating the use of oxygen in the cells.

DMSO (DiMethyl SulfOxide) - a solvent for reducing swelling and pain; enhances effectiveness of oxygen and other substances used in therapies.

Epstein Bar - a low immune system virus characterized by extreme fatigue, fever, sore throat, etc.

Free Radical - chemical compounds are comprised of two or more elements (atoms) joined by chemical *bonds*. These bonds are formed by electrons. A stable compound such as oxygen, has paired electrons. An unstable, reactive compound contains an unpaired electron. A highly reactive electron will seek out and attach itself to another electron to stabilize itself. A compound or element with an unpaired or extra electron is called a free radical.

Flora - bacteria in the intestine.

Germanium - a metalloid element with oxygen enhancing attributes.

Hippocrates - mathematician born 460 B.C. thought by some to be the father of medicine.

Lipids - fat soluble substance.

Orthodox medicine - conventional, allopathic, present day medical treatment.

Oxidation - a chemical reaction of oxygen. A process by which the body rids itself of waste.

Oxygen - a colorless, odorless, tasteless gas, forming about 20% by volume of the atmosphere, (O_2), and essential to life, etc.

Oxygenation - the act of impregnating, combining or supplying with oxygen.

Ozone - A very active, unstable form of oxygen with a peculiar, pungent odor. Containing three molecules of oxygen (O_3). A powerful oxidizing agent.

Ozone layer - A region of the stratosphere containing high concentrations of ozone, from 12-30 miles up.

Peroxide - A chemical compound containing two oxygen atoms, each of which is bonded to the other and to some other element other than oxygen, i.e.-hydrogen, magnesium, calcium.

Pathogens - a specific cause of disease, as a bacterium or virus.

Phospholipids - a complex substance in all living cells in association with stored fats.

Superoxygenation - abundant supply of oxygen.

Toxic waste - poisonous waste

Toxin - poison, pollutant, contaminant.

Bibliography

Ackerman, N. B.; Brinkley, F.B. Comparison of Effects on Tissue Oxygenation of Hyperbaric Oxygen and Intravascular Hydrogen Peroxide. Sur. 1968; 63:285-290.

Baker, Elizabeth. The UnDiet Book. San Diego, CA 92112, ProMotion Publishing, 1996.

Baker, Elizabeth; Baker, Dr. Elton. The UnCook Book. San Diego, CA 92112, ProMotion Publishing, 1996.

Baker, Elizabeth; Baker, Dr. Elton. The UnMedical Book. San Diego, CA 92112, ProMotion Publishing, 1996.

Balla, G. A.; Finney, J.W.; Aronoff, B.L., et al: Use of intra-arterial Hydrogen Peroxide to Promote Wound Healing. Amr. J. Surgery. 1964; 108:621-629.

Douglass, William Campbell, M.D. Hydrogen Peroxide Medical Miracle. Clayton, GA 30525. Valet Publishing, 1990.

Farr, C. H.: Physiological and Biochemical Responses to Intravenous Hydrogen Peroxide in Man. J. ACAM 1987; (In Press).

Farr, C. H.: The Therapeutic Use of Intravenous Hydrogen Peroxide (Monograph). Genesis Medical Center, Oklahoma City, OK 73120, Jan, 1987.

Fuson R. L.; Kylstra, J.A.; Hochslein, P., et al: Intravenous Hydrogen Peroxide Infusion as a means of Extrapulmonary Oxygenation. Clin. Res. 1967; 15:74.

McCabe, Ed. Oxygen Therapies. Morrisville, NY 13408,1990.

Nathan, C.F.; Cohn, Z.A.: <u>Antitumor Effects of Hydrogen Peroxide in Vivo</u>. J.Exp. Med. 1981; 154: 1539-1553.

Rilling, Siegfried, M.D.; Viebahn, Renate, Ph.D.: <u>The Use of Ozone in Medicine</u>. Heidelberg, Germany, Karl F. Haug Publishers, 1987.

ECHO, Newsletter, Spring 1994, Miami, FL 33138

Index

H

I

J

K

L

M

N

NHF—National Health Federation

To everyone who is interested in being in charge of their own health, I would like to tell you about the **National Health Federation**. NHF is a 39 year old educational and consumer rights organization, an advocate for your health freedoms.

I have been a member of the NHF for many years, have travelled to NHF shows across the U.S. to share my raw food experiences in workshops and lectures and to talk to many individuals like you who want to know more than they are being told.

My articles have been published in *"Health Freedom News,"* the NHF monthly magazine dedicated to keeping you abreast of the current developments on the political scene that affect your health rights, as well as vital and timely articles on self-help health care.

So I urge you with all my heart, to join the National Health Federation and become involved.

National Health Federation

P. O. BOX 688, Monrovia, CA 91017

Phone: 818-357-2181

Sincerely,

Elizabeth Baker